Real Estate
Dealmaking

A Property Investor's Guide
to NEGOTIATING

George F. Donohue

Dearborn™
Trade Publishing
A **Kaplan Professional** Company

This publication is designed to provide accurate and authoritative information in regard to the subject matter covered. It is sold with the understanding that the publisher is not engaged in rendering legal, accounting, or other professional service. If legal advice or other expert assistance is required, the services of a competent professional should be sought.

President, Dearborn Publishing: Roy Lipner
Vice President and Publisher: Cynthia A. Zigmund
Senior Acquisitions Editor: Mary B. Good
Development Editor: Karen Murphy
Senior Project Editor: Trey Thoelcke
Interior Design: Lucy Jenkins
Cover Design: Studio Montage
Typesetting: Janet Schroeder

Published by Dearborn Trade Publishing
A Kaplan Professional Company

Printed in the United States of America

05 06 07 10 9 8 7 6 5 4 3 2

Library of Congress Cataloging-in-Publication Data

Donohue, George F.
  Real estate dealmaking : a property investor's guide to negotiating / George F. Donohue.
     p. cm.
  Includes index.
  ISBN-13: 978-1-4195-2020-4
  1. Real estate business. 2. Negotiation in business. I. Title.
  HD1379.D62 2005
  333.33'068'4–dc22   2005015056

Dearborn Trade books are available at special quantity discounts to use for sales promotions, employee premiums, or educational purposes. Please call our Special Sales Department to order or for more information at 800-621-9621 ext. 4444, e-mail trade@dearborn.com, or write to Dearborn Trade Publishing, 30 South Wacker Drive, Suite 2500, Chicago, IL 60606-7481.

To my grandfather George F. Donohue I and my father George F. Donohue II. They taught me the value of ethics and treating all people with respect. They instilled in me the importance of conducting oneself in business with a sense of fair play and dignity. Through their encouragement I learned that a man's reputation is sacred.

To Robert Catlin, George Rossi, Charles Maikish, and Christian Deutsch—a few of the mentors I had the privilege to work with. Through hard work and practice, they taught me many of the effective tactics and techniques of negotiations.

To Trevor Glenn Donohue, my son. Through this book and my encouragement, I hope you will, one day, explore and understand the human dynamics required to be successful in negotiating and happy in life.

Contents

To live is to negotiate. Everyone negotiates for something every day. People negotiate for items from the simplest to the most important things in their lives. The purchase of a home or any other type of property, for example, is a major event in a person's life. For many people, this purchase is one of the most important negotiations they'll ever have.

You'll find that the better you negotiate, the better your life will be. I've observed that those who are adept at negotiating live more confidently and with less stress than novice negotiators. Because of that skill, they usually gain an advantage in all the opportunities that they pursue.

To improve your negotiating skills, this book provides training, guidelines, tips, and tactics on how to become a better negotiator. Remember, the trained negotiator who has a well-thought-out plan will always do better against someone who has not prepared and is a novice at negotiating.

WHY PEOPLE FEAR NEGOTIATION

Commonly, people don't feel good about negotiating because they're filled with fear. In my seminars, people share what their biggest negotiating fears are. See if any of these sound familiar: being taken advantage of, being unprepared, not having the skills, losing money on a bad deal, being too rigid or too aggressive, paying too much, not getting enough money, not having enough confidence to negotiate, and so on. People often fear negotiation because they simply don't have enough experience.

This book can't give you firsthand experience, but it will help you understand the nuances of negotiation and build understanding through examples, exercises, and role-plays.

NEGOTIATION: A WIN-WIN FOR ALL

Some people want to learn about negotiation to find out how to get an advantage over another at the negotiation table. From their point of view, it's all about "getting the most." That's considered to be a win-lose scenario.

I've got news for you: Negotiation is not about maximizing *you*. That's the first thing you need to realize. Professional negotiators understand and live and breathe this truth. Rather, negotiation revolves around satisfying the majority of needs for *all* parties.

Some people define negotiation as a compromise, or a give-and-take. I define it as *an exchange of information and ideas for the purpose of reaching a mutually accepted decision.*

Consider the other person's motivations, goals, and needs. The negotiation process takes them into account to produce a "meeting of the minds." In fact, "meeting of the minds" is a legal term used by real estate brokers because it means they get paid when two parties have a meeting of the minds—that is, when they've negotiated an agreement that successfully meets the majority of their needs. Simply stated, in real estate negotiations, "meeting of the minds" constitutes a commissionable event.

To set up a win-win situation, all parties communicate their respective goal or goals. Keep in mind the three Cs: conviction, clarity, and confidence. In this context:

- *Conviction* means having strong persuasion or a strong belief. This require's negotiating with *conviction* to lead your opponent into a state of being convinced.
- *Clarity* means negotiating with clear, precise, accurate communication. It is imperative that your negotiations are carried out with *clarity* so everyone understands the agreements all parties have reached.
- *Confidence* means to have a feeling of one's power over one's circumstance. Through proper planning, you will be able to successfully negotiate each step of the way with *confidence*.

SPECIFIC TOOLS AND TACTICS

In this book, you'll move from a general definition of negotiation to specific tools and tactics. This structure will give you the basic foundation of the purpose of negotiating and a general outline of good negotiating strategies. The chapters are arranged according to the order in which people meet and deal with each other through a typical real estate negotiation process.

This book also includes many tables and charts to help you before and during your negotiation. In addition to using these, take the time to create your own tables and keep them in your computer or in some other handy reference place. You never know when you will need to negotiate, so have your tools nearby.

An important chapter on role-playing (Chapter 15, supplemented by Appendix G) is designed to get you to practice your newly acquired negotiation skills. Before becoming familiar with the process of using role-playing to practice negotiating, most people think that it will be an awkward experience. However, I urge you to try all of the role-playing scenarios I've included in this book and more! Once you begin to carry out the role-playing with your friends and colleagues, you'll get the hang of it and enjoy the interaction, while gaining valuable experience for your real estate transactions.

TWOFOLD APPROACH

Here's my suggestion for getting the most from this book. Read it completely through in one or two sittings. Absorb the general points from each chapter and the overall philosophy of negotiating represented throughout this book. Then, once you're in a real negotiation situation or about to begin one, reread the chapter or chapters that best apply to that particular point in the negotiation. I also suggest you pay special attention to the graphs—they provide "pictures" that will make the negotiation process easier to understand.

Good luck and enjoy the negotiating journey every step of the way!

Thank you to the thousands of people I have negotiated with around the world over the past 28 years. You have given me the practical experience that has honed my negotiating skills.

I thank Samantha Del Canto and The Learning Annex of New York for their generous support of this book.

I greatly appreciate the wonderful editorial help from of Barbara McNichol, assisted by Sherry Sterling.

I am thankful for all the help from Mary B. Good and Leslie Banks of Dearborn Trade Publishing.

Special thanks to Tami for her encouragement and understanding.

1

NEGOTIATION VERSUS
SUCCESSFUL NEGOTIATION

You can never learn less; you can only learn more.

Buckminster Fuller

"It's not about you," I stress to every student and new employee I teach in my negotiating classes. You can simply negotiate or you can *successfully* negotiate. There is a difference.

Untrained negotiators always find themselves at a disadvantage. Just imagine trying to compete at an athletic game or a chess match without knowing how to play well. You pit your short amount of training against a well-trained, experienced opponent. Of course, you always can rely on the phenomenon of "beginner's luck." But do you really want to take a chance when it comes to negotiating details about such an important part of your life—the purchase of a home or an investment property?

A highly trained negotiator understands the importance of having a plan that contains various alternatives, ready to be used to your advantage at a moment's notice (see Chapter 3, Your Negotiation Plan). For example, if two investors were seeking to purchase the same property, the one who is a trained negotiator would have many basic advantages over an inexperienced negotiator. The trained negotiator would

- be able to determine the specific reason for the sale,
- have alternatives ready in a typewritten plan,

- know how to conduct research on all aspects of the negotiation,
- be prepared to overcome any objection or obstacle,
- be able to use other professionals appropriately,
- understand how to use flexibility as a strength,
- know how to prepare a priority list and sequence of negotiating topics,
- have strategies designed to meet deadlines in place,
- have the awareness to discern the weakness of the other side, and
- know when to use the technique of silence.

Think of the untrained negotiator as an untrained hiker lost in a forest with no compass, no provisions, and no map. That doesn't make for a pleasant hike and could even be dangerous. Would you prefer to be the one who comes prepared or the one who gets lost in the forest?

WIN-WIN OBJECTIVE

As noted in the Preface, successful negotiating focuses on satisfying all parties, not on maximizing your own stance. Therefore, this book is not about how to perfect an aggressive win-everything attitude, especially when it comes to such big-ticket items as real estate properties. You can be assured that many sophisticated buyers and sellers know the chess game of negotiations. My tips and techniques will help you to contend with all the characters you meet in a transaction. In fact, I recommend that you carry out all of the tips and strategies explained in this book with a high level of courteousness, professionalism, and respect. Not only is this style of negotiating most effective, it also will reinforce your confidence and earn you respect and admiration from the people you want to work with in the real estate industry.

Know that negotiating is *not* about the property; it's about the people. You negotiate *with* and *against* people, not with the real estate property itself. Which people will you have to negotiate with? Your partner, bankers, real estate brokers, lawyers, sellers, general contractors, property managers or tenants, inspectors, and more. The people in each of these roles have different motivations and different interests that require you to employ a variety of negotiating tactics. You'll learn these from studying this book and through lots of practice, practice, practice.

VISUALIZATION/PROJECTION

I genuinely enjoy training young real estate professionals in the art of negotiating. Sometimes the day before an important negotiation, I will ask a few of the junior brokers scheduled to be at the negotiation session to come see me in my office. I don't tell them the nature of my request because I want to determine how much preparation they already have made for the upcoming negotiation. I'll ask them to sit down and tell me, as best as they can, exactly what they expect to happen in the next day's meeting. In response, they usually give me a quizzical, confused stare. From there, I proceed to help them visualize or project what will happen in the negotiation session by asking these questions:

- In tomorrow's negotiation, who will open up the session?
- What will be the first question asked by our team?
- How will the other side answer that question?
- Which of our opponents will be leading the negotiation?
- What will be the second most important topic we will cover?
- How will the other side reply to that topic?
- What will be the toughest question they will ask us?
- What is the toughest question we will ask them?
- From our point of view, how many components to the deal are there?
- How many components do you think they will bring up in the discussion?
- What will be the last topic we discuss?

Usually, first-time junior negotiators think I'm crazy when I go through this visualization session with them. It is only later, after they've acquired some negotiation battle scars, that they begin to appreciate this exercise of projection.

Quite often the night before an important negotiation, I find a place in my home to sit in solitude for an hour or two. In this quiet space, I visualize the actual negotiation just as if I were imagining a complete chess game. I can almost hear my opponent's replies to each of my questions and recommendations. I can see in my mind's eye how I am putting all of my tactics into the negotiation strategy.

I find this kind of preparation valuable, and you will, too. Over time, hone your ability to project and visualize the negotiation in your mind the night before, then confidently and with conviction, you can clearly orchestrate your plan the next day.

LEARNING FROM HOSTAGE NEGOTIATORS

Negotiating takes place in many arenas other than in the world of real estate. One example is the type used in hostage negotiations. Although the two kinds are inherently different, a few elements of hostage negotiations cross over with real estate negotiations. I believe that studying these elements can strengthen your skills and awareness.

Consider what components come into play for law enforcement officers and others who handle hostage negotiations and see how you might use these skills in your real estate negotiations. General negotiation methods you can apply are:

- Emotion labeling, or attaching a tentative label to the feelings expressed or implied by the subject's words or actions.
- Paraphrasing, reflecting, or mirroring to indicate the ability to see things from the subject's perspective by repeating the last words or the main ideas of the subject's message in your own words.
- Asking open-ended questions that stimulate the subject to talk rather than asking questions that elicit one-word answers.
- Validating facts by putting what is known on the table.

Some methods to use at the crisis stage are:

- Active listening to establish common ground, be alert for suicidal or homicidal behaviors, and prevent acting out.
- Probing the cause of the problem to add reassurance and overcome communication impasses.
- Using I/we content information to establish credibility.

- Expressing concern about their low-level needs, as defined by Maslow's Hierarchy of Needs (see next page), to encourage safety.
- Using pauses and clarifying meaning to help identify core problems.
- Clarifying feelings to validate their feelings.

During the negotiation stage:

- Asking problem-oriented questions to help predict outcomes and possible consequences, and to eliminate unacceptable solutions.
- Identifying advantages to encourage finding a solution.
- Continued use of I/we content information to facilitate planning a different solution.
- Summarizing solutions and using a command structure to get to the point of being ready to implement a plan.

During the solution stage:

- Using guided viewing to resolve the problem.
- Practicing stress management and mediation procedures to defuse the situation for everyone involved.

Similar Components in Real Estate

Of these components used for hostage negotiations, notice that the following ones are particularly important in real estate negotiations:

- Establish common ground
- Probe causes
- Establish credibility
- Identify and assess problems
- Validate facts
- Use active listening
- Clarify meanings
- Facilitate prediction of outcome and consequences
- Facilitate the planning of different solutions

In addition, two more important similarities used by top hostage negotiators are key components in real estate negotiations:

1. Top hostage negotiators have trained well and are capable of creating a negotiating plan and carrying it out. (See Chapter 3.)
2. Top hostage negotiators continually participate in role-playing to sharpen their negotiating skills. (See Chapter 15.)

Maslow's Hierarchy of Needs

It is interesting to note the mention of Maslow's Hierarchy of Needs in this discussion about hostage negotiations. Abraham Maslow established his well-accepted theory of a hierarchy of needs for all human beings. He believed that human beings are motivated by unsatisfied needs and that certain lower-level needs must be satisfied before higher-level needs can be satisfied. It's easy to see the correlation of basic needs to the negotiation process; that is, certain crucial needs and requirements must be satisfied before other requirements.

The hostage negotiation list also cites active listening. Active listening is the ability to listen to someone's comments, offer suggestions, and acknowledge that you hear him or her by repeating the person's sentiments or rephrasing what has just been said or simply stating, "I understand."

SUMMARY POINTS FOR CHAPTER 1: NEGOTIATION VERSUS *SUCCESSFUL* NEGOTIATION

- Trained negotiators have many basic advantages over inexperienced negotiators.
- A highly trained negotiator understands the importance of having a plan that contains various alternatives.
- You negotiate *with* and *against* people, not with the real estate property itself. These people include your partner or partners, bankers, real estate brokers, lawyers, sellers, general contractors, property managers or tenants, inspectors, and more.

- Taking time to visualize the details of an upcoming negotiation just as if you were imagining playing a complete chess game is a valuable practice in learning to achieve what you want.
- Several important components of hostage negotiations can apply when negotiating real estate deals. Studying hostage negotiations can strengthen your skills and awareness for your real estate negotiations.
- In negotiations, as in life, certain crucial needs must be satisfied before other requirements can be met, as Maslow's Hierarchy of Needs indicates.
- It's important to clarify what you believe your opponent's proposal is by repeating its elements.

2

THE IMPORTANCE OF BEING PREPARED

The more complicated and powerful the job, the more rudimentary the preparation for it.

William F. Buckley, Jr.

Because the negotiation process begins well before the actual appointment you make to close a deal, it's critical that you prepare a well-thought-out plan before you begin any type of real estate conciliation. This requires gathering information about all the others involved, the topics you will be discussing in the negotiation, and the market where that particular real estate property is located. But gathering information is not enough; it also is essential that you validate the information that you have obtained.

Each negotiation session should be viewed as an important, short (only two to three hours) event, similar in length to an opera, a football game, or a courtroom trial. Although these special events only last a couple of hours, the number of hours required to prepare for them is enormous. Similarly, the preparation ratio for a negotiation session should be closer to 10:1 rather than 1:1. That means a skilled negotiator will spend ten hours of preparation to get ready for a one-hour negotiation session. If you can schedule negotiation sessions several days to one week apart, it will give you the ability to spend two to three solid hours a day to prepare for them extremely well.

Trust but **V**alidate

At my firm, we close every sales meeting with the expression, "Trust but validate." This basic business philosophy is key in negotiating. Each step of the way of the negotiation process, it's essential—imperative—to ask for the information you receive to be validated.

A well-trained, professional negotiator projects a demeanor of trust. Showing that your trust is not being naïve nor is it showing a sign of weakness. However, you trust in your opponent should always be kept in check. Politely validating everything will modulate your trust toward your opponent.

For example, if your opponent apprises you verbally on expenses of a property you may buy, you should reply, "That sounds reasonable. Would you mind sending me the past six months of bills so I can become more familiar with the details?" If the information you're validating consistently matches the information that's verbally provided, it clearly indicates that your opponent can be trusted in this negotiation.

IT'S NOT IN WRITING? IT DIDN'T HAPPEN!

Quite a few times, a young real estate broker has walked into my office lamenting about a deal that had seemed to be going well from his point of view. Then that deal unexpectedly died. In my experience, the root of situations like this has always been a young broker's indifference to *memorializing,* or documenting, the negotiation as it progresses. I always stress the importance of writing things down and sending copies to *all* the interested parties in the negotiation at every juncture.

It's human nature for people to hear what they want to hear. They have a lot of things on their minds, especially if they're working a full-time job and also trying to negotiate real estate deals. Your opponents may not retain as much information or remember as many agreements as you think they do. You may have misunderstood one point or perhaps forgotten another point. Most people don't like to write down the highlights of a discussion along the way because, they complain, it takes too much time. The reality is that by memorializing each step of the way, it improves the negotiation *and* gives you negotiating strength. That way, in your letters to the other parties, you can prioritize the elements you communicate the way you see fit.

Makes a Good Deal of Common Sense

I am often amazed when I hear mature adults advising young investors to never put anything in writing. Somehow, they think this will create leverage. I believe it's the coward's way to negotiate. If you and your opponent have had a discussion in which you have agreed on some points, disagreed on other points, and tabled certain items for a later discussion—but agreed to still carry on the negotiations—it makes a great deal of common sense to memorialize those points and share them immediately.

I also find sending these types of letters back and forth in a negotiation provides me with clarity. Through the exercise of summarizing the discussions, I review the points again and relive the negotiation on paper. It also gives me the opportunity to see the whole negotiation thus far in summary form.

It's true, writing down every piece of the negotiation takes time. But in the long run, it will save you a great deal of time and dollars in miscommunication and perhaps legal expenses.

Speaking of legal expenses, another important reason to document everything is for protection from litigation. Remember, your goal is to arrive at a mutually satisfactory agreement. However, especially in high-stakes real estate, the parties may end up in litigation because one of the parties did not adhere to what was agreed on.

You then may find yourself in a different type of negotiation related to real estate—the negotiation of litigation. Therefore, having thorough, clearly written, dated material from your negotiation sessions will give you a powerful advantage over the other parties in the event you find yourself in litigation.

INDISPUTABLES—A TOOL
IN NEGOTIATIONS

One critical strategy in negotiating also employs writing down the negotiation plan and proposals. Whenever I negotiate, I strive to make statements that are indisputable because being able to declare an "indisputable" can prove to be a powerful tool in the negotiation process.

An "indisputable" is a statement that defines a situation or fact that no one in the negotiation room can dispute. These statements are made during the negotiation process to gain an advantage, and can be used from both ends of the negotiation table—either when you're on the offensive or when you need to defend your position. Indisputables should be rehearsed, even written down, so in the heat of the negotiation you can articulate them with confidence.

Seek to Declare "Indisputables"

Have you ever been in the presence of someone who has made a thought-provoking statement followed by people looking at one another and nodding in agreement that what the person just said cannot be disputed? That person most likely knows the subject thoroughly and has conducted a great deal of research to speak so confidently.

You can negotiate in the same way. Prepare and plan your strategy like a good chess player and be prepared to declare your "indisputable" at the right moment. When your opponent states, "You're right," you know you've succeeded in declaring an indisputable.

For example, you may have statistics published by an unbiased third party that cite the price of a certain type of property has declined in the past two years and likely will continue to decline in the next six months. During the negotiations, you may want to place these statistics in front of your opponent, stating, "Prices on your kind of building are going down and they appear to continue to do so. Please take a look at this." Then you'd show him or her the "indisputable" evidence you gathered about the market.

Sometimes, you'll need to lead your opponent into a discussion where you can declare an indisputable. If properly done, it will give you the same powerful feeling as declaring "checkmate" at the end of a chess match.

Example of "Checkmating" Your Opponent

Let's say Jack is selling a property you want to purchase. He has provided you with the income and expense numbers for that property. You further investigate the income and expenses listed to be sure all items are included. From that, you calculate the property's net operating income, which is gross income minus expenses.

One way you determine the value of the property is by dividing the net operating income by a rate of return, or ROI, that you deem acceptable. For example:

$$Income = \$48,000$$
$$Expenses = \underline{\ 30,000}$$
$$Net\ operating\ income = \$18,000$$

An acceptable rate of return might be 6 percent (.06).
Therefore, the value is calculated as follows:

$$\frac{18,000}{.06} = \$300.000$$

Jack is asking $360,000 for the property. Given that, you ask him, "What do you think is an acceptable rate of return for an investment like this?" You want to get Jack to answer 6 percent or greater. If he says 6 percent, you must immediately recite your "indisputable" statement: "Well, if you believe an investment should return 6 percent, then this property is only worth $300,000. Let me show you. The income is $48,000, expenses are $30,000, and therefore the net operating income is $18,000. What is $18,000 divided by 6 percent?" Then hand your calculator to Jack and let him do the calculation. Checkmate!

DO RESEARCH BEFORE WRITING A NEGOTIATION PLAN

Before you write a negotiation plan to purchase a property (see the sample negotiation plan in Chapter 3), start by deciding what type of information you will require. For negotiations in real estate, I suggest you thoroughly research some or all of the following information:

- Trends in home sales
- Forecasts of home sales
- History of interest rates
- Supply and demand for housing
- Rate of inflation
- Laws that affect real estate
- Return on investment (ROI) for alternative investments (that is, if you put the same money into stocks and bonds instead of this property, what would be a likely return on your investment and is it better?)
- Unemployment rate

Let's look at each of these in detail.

Trends in Home Sales

Trends are essential to understand because they help you make decisions and, if properly used, aid in your negotiations. Make sure you bring data on trends to the negotiation table, preferably "indisputable" data.

You can look up trends for home sales in the following places:

- Real estate broker Web sites
- Real estate publications
- Newspapers, such as *The Wall Street Journal* and *The New York Times*
- The Commerce Department of the U.S. government
- Local government offices
- Harvard University's Joint Center for Housing Studies
- The National Association of Realtors
- The National Association of Home Builders
- The Center for Economic and Policy Research in Washington, D.C.

Forecasts of Home Sales

Information on forecasts, or "future looking," can be found through the same sources mentioned above. However, a person's ability to forecast should always be taken with a grain of salt. That said, some of the largest accounting firms are excellent sources of information related to real estate. They include the following:

- Ernst & Young produces the real estate market outlook and other reports on real estate investment opportunities. (http://www.ey.com)
- PricewaterhouseCoopers, another well-known firm, publishes *Emerging Trends in Real Estate*. (http://www.pwcglobal.com)
- KPMG has published real estate reports for many years. (http://www.kpmg.com)
- Deloitte & Touche USA is another well-known firm that has tracked real estate in numerous markets. (http://www.deloitte.com)

You're wise to study the publications available through these firms because they show periodic forecasts of most major markets in the United States and abroad. You can use the information in determining if you want certain properties and how much they're likely to be worth in the future.

History of Interest Rates

Interest rates are important to understand because they directly affect real estate. To be specific, each time the prime interest rate increases, it means fewer people can afford mortgages. For example, if interest rates in the marketplace rose to 7 percent from 6 percent, then the monthly payment for a $250,000 mortgage would increase by $170—from approximately $1,500 a month to $1,670 a month.

Do you see how each increase helps reduce the overall demand to purchase homes? In addition, higher interest rates keep renters living in rental properties instead of buying their own homes. This provides an advantage to those who own rental property—namely, you.

You can obtain detailed information on interest rates from the following:

- Federal Reserve Bank (http://www.federalreserve.gov)
- Various banks and mortgage companies (look on their Web sites)
- Mortgage Bankers Association (http://www.wmba.org)

FIGURE 2.1 *U.S. Interest Rates Since 1998*

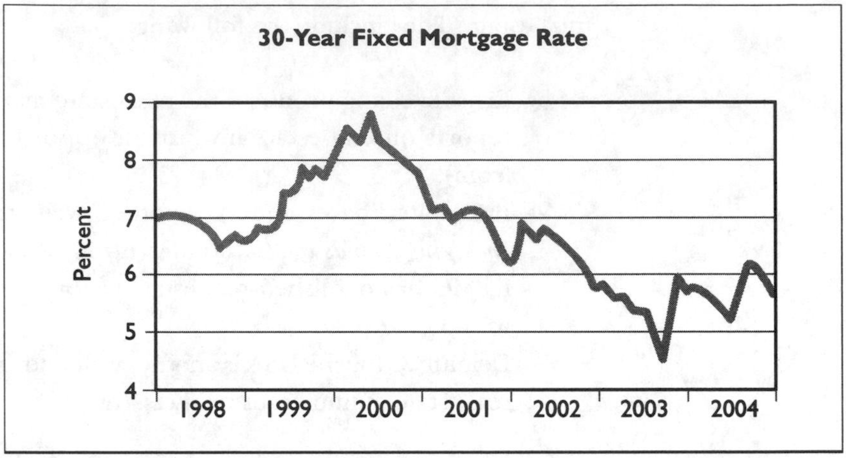

30-Year Fixed Mortgage Rate

Source: U.S. Bureau of Labor Statistics

In Figure 2.1, you can see how interest rates have fared in the United States for 30-year fixed-rate mortgage loans since 1998.

Supply and Demand for Housing

Obtaining information about the current supply and demand of properties can be tricky. No single place for finding supply and demand information at a particular locale exists, so be prepared to do some creative research.

On the supply side, primarily look for information that tracks the amount of a particular type of property in a specific area and focus your research accordingly. For example, you may want to find information about how many three-bedroom homes exist in a particular zip code. You can obtain this information from a real estate broker who has access to the multiple listing service (MLS) and other real estate databases.

Of course, you also can obtain information on the demand side from a real estate broker. The broker should be able to tell you how many three-bedroom homes were sold compared to other types of homes and as a percentage of three-bedroom homes that exist in a particular zip code.

FIGURE 2.2 *Median and Average Sales Prices of New Homes Sold in the United States*

Annual Data		
Period	**Median**	**Average**
1963	$18,000	$19,300
1964	18,900	20,500
1965	20,000	21,500
1966	21,400	23,300
1967	22,700	24,600
1968	24,700	26,600
1969	25,600	27,900
1970	23,400	26,600
1971	25,200	28,300
1972	27,600	30,500
1973	32,500	35,500
1974	35,900	38,900
1975	39,300	42,600
1976	44,200	48,000
1977	48,800	54,200
1978	55,700	62,500
1979	62,900	71,800
1980	64,600	76,400
1981	68,900	83,000
1982	69,300	83,900
1983	75,300	89,800
1984	79,900	97,600
1985	84,300	100,800
1986	92,000	111,900
1987	104,500	127,200
1988	112,500	138,300
1989	120,000	148,800
1990	122,900	149,800
1991	120,000	147,200
1992	121,500	144,100
1993	126,500	147,700
1994	130,000	154,500
1995	133,900	158,700
1996	140,000	166,400
1997	146,000	176,200
1998	152,500	181,900
1999	161,000	195,600
2000	169,000	207,000
2001	175,200	213,200
2002	187,600	228,700
2003	195,000	246,300

Note: The sales price includes the land.

FIGURE 2.3 *Median and Average New Homes Sold in the United States*

Period	U.S.	Northeast	Midwest	South	West
Annual Data					
Sold during period (not seasonally adjusted)					
1963	560	87	134	199	141
1964	565	90	146	200	129
1965	575	94	142	210	129
1966	461	84	113	166	99
1967	487	77	112	179	119
1968	490	73	119	177	121
1969	448	62	97	175	114
1970	485	61	100	203	121
1971	656	82	127	270	176
1972	718	96	130	305	187
1973	634	95	120	257	161
1974	519	69	103	207	139
1975	549	71	106	222	150
1976	646	72	128	247	199
1977	819	86	162	317	255
1978	817	78	145	331	262
1979	709	67	112	304	225
1980	545	50	81	267	145
1981	436	46	60	219	112
1982	412	47	48	219	99
1983	623	76	71	323	52
1984	639	94	76	309	160
1985	688	112	82	323	171
1986	750	136	96	322	196
1987	671	117	97	271	186
1988	676	101	97	276	202
1989	650	86	102	260	202
1990	534	71	89	225	149
1991	509	57	93	215	144
1992	610	65	116	259	170
1993	666	60	123	295	188
1994	670	61	123	295	191
1995	667	55	125	300	187
1996	757	74	137	337	209

FIGURE 2.3 *Median and Average New Homes Sold in the United States*

Annual Data
Sold during period (not seasonally adjusted)

Period	U.S.	Northeast	Midwest	South	West
1997	804	78	140	363	223
1998	886	81	164	398	243
1999	880	76	168	395	242
2000	877	71	155	406	244
2001	908	66	164	439	239
2002	973	65	185	450	273
2003	1,086	79	189	511	307
2004	1,202	83	210	562	347

Note: Estimates prior to 1999 include an upward adjustment of 3.3 percent made to account for houses sold in permit-issuing areas that will never have a permit authorization.
(Components may not add to total because of rounding. Number of housing units in thousands.)

Rate of Inflation

Certainly the value of the dollar affects the value of property and inflation cuts into those values over time. That's why it's important to take into account the future value of money as it's affected by inflation.

Figure 2.5 shows the historic rise of inflation over the past nine decades.

Laws That Affect Real Estate

Real estate laws don't change that often. However, it's important to keep your finger on the pulse of laws that could affect real estate in your area. For example, you might find a seller willing to sell an office building for what appears to be below-market price. Little do you know that a new law requiring all building owners to install water sprinklers throughout their buildings passed recently. The cost of putting in sprinklers through a whole building is enormous. In this example, that's the motivation behind selling the building for such a low price.

FIGURE 2.4 *Median and Average Sales Prices of Houses Sold by Region*

Period	Median Sales Price					Average Sales Price				
	U.S.	Northeast	Midwest	South	West	U.S.	Northeast	Midwest	South	West
1963	$18,000	$20,300	$17,900	$16,100	$18,800	$19,300	$22,300	$19,700	$16,800	$20,800
1964	18,900	20,300	19,400	16,700	20,400	20,500	21,800	20,700	18,100	23,200
1965	20,000	21,500	21,600	17,500	21,600	21,500	22,900	22,800	18,900	23,200
1966	21,400	23,500	23,200	18,200	23,200	23,300	25,200	24,600	20,200	25,500
1967	22,700	25,400	25,100	19,400	24,100	24,600	27,700	26,400	21,100	26,100
1968	24,700	27,700	27,400	21,500	25,100	26,600	30,100	28,500	23,600	27,100
1969	25,600	31,600	27,600	22,800	25,300	27,900	33,400	29,900	25,300	27,400
1970	23,400	30,300	24,400	20,300	24,000	26,600	32,800	28,000	24,000	26,900
1971	25,200	30,600	27,200	22,500	25,500	28,300	34,400	29,900	5,900	28,000
1972	27,600	31,400	29,300	25,800	27,500	30,500	35,700	31,400	28,500	30,500
1973	32,500	37,100	32,900	30,900	32,400	35,500	40,600	36,700	33,200	35,300
1974	35,900	40,100	36,100	34,500	35,800	38,900	43,700	39,300	36,800	39,300
1975	39,300	44,000	9,600	37,300	40,600	42,600	47,000	43,400	39,600	44,300
1976	44,200	47,300	4,800	40,500	47,200	48,000	50,000	48,600	3,800	51,900
1977	48,800	51,600	51,500	44,100	53,500	54,200	54,800	55,200	48,100	60,700
1978	55,700	58,100	59,200	50,300	61,300	62,500	63,000	64,200	55,600	70,100
1979	62,900	65,500	3,900	57,300	69,600	71,800	71,500	73,000	63,800	82,000
1980	64,600	69,500	63,400	59,600	72,300	76,400	80,300	74,400	69,100	89,400
1981	68,900	76,000	65,900	64,400	77,800	83,000	88,500	82,500	75,600	95,800
1982	69,300	78,200	68,900	66,100	75,000	83,900	88,600	87,700	78,300	92,600
1983	75,300	82,200	79,500	70,900	80,100	89,800	96,200	97,600	83,000	97,200

FIGURE 2.4 *Median and Average Sales Prices of Houses Sold by Region*

Period	Median Sales Price					Average Sales Price				
	U.S.	Northeast	Midwest	South	West	U.S.	Northeast	Midwest	South	West
1984	79,900	88,600	85,400	2,000	87,300	97,600	107,400	107,800	86,000	109,400
1985	84,300	103,300	80,300	75,000	92,600	100,800	121,900	95,400	88,900	111,800
1986	92,000	125,000	88,300	80,200	95,700	111,900	151,300	102,600	95,300	116,100
1987	104,500	140,000	95,000	88,000	111,000	127,200	170,900	115,500	106,600	134,600
1988	112,500	149,000	101,600	92,000	126,500	138,300	179,300	123,700	114,800	155,700
1989	120,000	159,600	108,800	96,400	139,000	148,800	188,600	130,600	123,100	173,900
1990	122,900	159,000	107,900	99,000	147,500	149,800	190,500	133,000	123,500	180,600
1991	120,000	155,900	110,000	100,000	141,100	147,200	188,800	134,500	123,000	176,400
1992	121,500	169,000	115,600	105,500	130,400	144,100	194,900	136,400	126,900	157,800
1993	126,500	162,600	125,000	115,000	135,000	147,700	183,600	143,100	133,600	161,900
1994	130,000	169,000	132,900	116,900	140,400	154,500	200,500	152,700	36,800	168,900
1995	133,900	180,000	134,000	124,500	141,000	158,700	16,600	157,200	142,000	169,800
1996	140,000	186,900	137,500	25,000	153,900	166,400	226,800	158,100	143,100	185,900
1997	146,000	190,000	149,900	129,600	160,000	176,200	234,100	173,000	151,400	198,200
1998	152,500	200,000	157,500	135,800	163,500	181,900	240,100	179,200	159,700	200,500
1999	161,000	210,500	164,000	145,900	173,700	195,600	247,900	186,800	73,000	221,700
2000	169,000	227,400	169,700	148,000	196,400	207,000	274,800	199,300	179,000	238,900
2001	175,200	246,400	172,600	155,400	213,600	213,200	294,300	201,300	185,700	250,000
2002	187,600	264,300	178,000	163,400	238,500	228,700	301,300	209,800	197,500	276,500
2003	195,000	264,500	184,300	168,100	260,900	246,300	315,700	218,200	208,900	306,800
2003	218,900	312,000	203,400	78,500	79,300	272,500	362,200	239,500	228,800	338,900

FIGURE 2.5 *Yearly Inflation/Deflation Rate, 1915–2002*

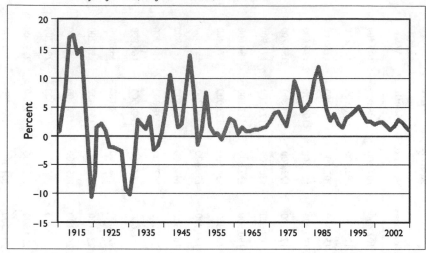

For information regarding real estate law, I suggest reviewing the following Web sites:

- http://www.findlaw.com—a Web site for legal professionals
- http://www.real-estate-law.freeadvice.com

Return on Investment (ROI) for Alternative Investments

The concept of a return on investment can be a complicated matter. For our purposes, it's important that the negotiator understand what the possible return on investment could be from the desired real estate and compare it to non–real estate investments, such as stocks and bonds.

Getting ready for a negotiation meeting, you need to determine what type of return you are seeking. To put things in perspective, first examine certificate of deposit (CD) statistics. (See Figure 2.6, The History of CD Rates.) The return on a bank CD is quite low today. However, look at CDs in the year 1981. If you had simply put your cash in a bank CD, you would have realized an annual rate of return on your money greater than 15 percent—with no hassle! Real estate investors in the early 2000s would be ecstatic if they could achieve anywhere close to that percentage.

In your negotiations, you may want to use statistics to compare the ROI of other types of investments against a real estate investment. For example, you may want to draw a comparison between the property you

FIGURE 2.6 *The History of CD Rates*

The rate on CDs is a simple average of dealer rates on negotiable CDs nationally traded in the secondary market. Rates are determined for each business day. Following is a history of CD rates since 1964:

Year	Rate	Year	Rate	Year	Rate	Year	Rate
1964	4.03%	1975	6.90%	1986	6.50%	1997	5.73%
1965	4.45	1976	5.63	1987	7.0	1998	5.44
1966	5.60	1977	5.91	1988	7.91	1999	5.46
1967	5.19	1978	8.60	1989	9.08	2000	6.59
1968	5.97	1979	11.42	1990	8.17	2001	3.66
1969	7.34	1980	12.94	1991	5.91	2002	1.81
1970	7.64	1981	15.79	1992	3.76	2003	1.17
1971	5.21	1982	12.57	1993	3.28	2004	1.74
1972	5.01	1983	9.28	1994	4.96		
1973	9.05	1984	10.71	1995	5.98		
1974	10.02	1985	8.24	1996	5.47		

wish to purchase and investing in a particular stock offered by certain companies. I suggest you compare the ROI or yield from the stock dividend with the yield from a real estate investment.

To calculate the yield, take the dividend amount and divide it by the stock price. For example, if a stock pays the dividend of $1.50 and the stock price is $25, the dividend yield is 6 percent.

You can use this information in a negotiation in this way: "After analyzing the income and expenses of your property, Sam Smith determined the return (ROI) would be approximately 6 percent per year. As you know, I could invest in a rather stable stock and obtain the same 6 percent dividend yield. The price you are asking is not very attractive compared to other investments I can put my money into."

Unemployment Rate

The unemployment rate can be an indicator of the economic viability of an area you invest in. If unemployment is going down, that could mean more companies are moving into an area and are seeking to rent office space or retail space. It also means that more people with jobs can afford homes.

FIGURE 2.7 *U.S. Unemployment Rate 1993–2004*

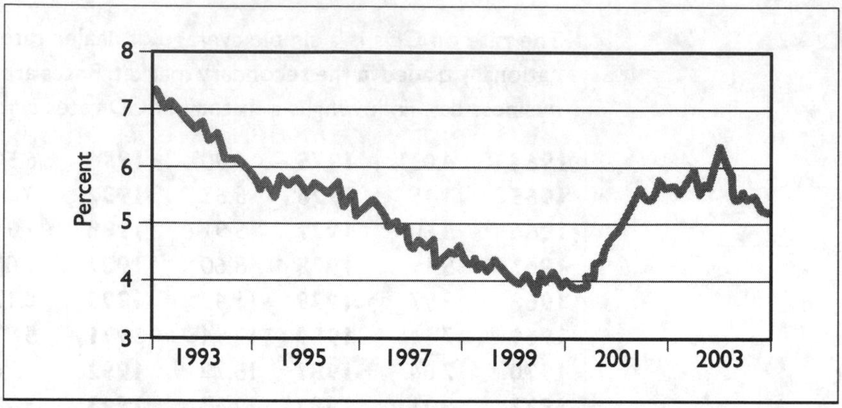

Source: U.S. Bureau of Labor Statistics

If, on the other hand, unemployment is increasing, landlords could be losing tenants—both commercial and residential. Often when a building's occupancy rate decreases, its value also decreases.

Unemployment rate information can be obtained from the following:

- U.S. Department of Labor, Bureau of Labor Statistics (http://www.bls.gov)
- Local state and city government Web sites

Figure 2.7 shows the history of unemployment in the United States since 1993.

RESEARCH FOR COMMERCIAL REAL ESTATE

For real estate that has a commercial component including office and retail space, you also may gather data on:

- Vacancy rates
- Rental rates
- Absorption rates
- Fastest-growing businesses

Vacancy Rates

Vacancy rates tell an important story regarding the marketplace. If the vacancy rates of commercial buildings are dropping and it appears they'll continue to drop, the value of the properties could decrease. Logically, if fewer tenants are paying the rent, less money is available to pay the expenses. Remember, the net operating income of a property is tied to its value. That means the less income that a property throws off while its expenses remain the same, the less its value.

You can obtain information about vacancy rates in the United States from these sources:

- U.S. Department of Commerce (http://www.doc.gov)
- U.S. Census Bureau (http://www.census.gov)
- National Association of Realtors (http://www.realtor.com)
- REIS Inc. (http://www.reis.com)
- International Council of Shopping Centers (http://www.icsc.org)
- Commercial real estate publications
- The real estate boards of various states in the United States

Rental Rates

Rental rate information can be obtained from the same sources used to find vacancy rates. However, major real estate brokerage companies in a particular geographical area will track rental rates more closely and frequently than many of the national ones. One example is the CBRE's MarketView of Midtown Manhattan (http://www.cbre.com).

Absorption Rates

Absorption refers to the amount of property that is being sold (or absorbed). Absorption rates can be obtained from the major real estate brokerage companies in the particular area you are seeking to purchase or sell a property in. An example would be the U.S. Department of Housing and Urban Development's report of Market Absorption of Apartments, available from the U.S. Census Bureau.

Fastest-Growing Businesses

The best place to find the fastest-growing businesses is *Inc.* magazine (http://www.inc.com), which publishes a periodic list of the fastest-growing businesses and the local municipality of where the property is located.

In addition, some local government offices and chambers of commerce have economic development committees or departments that track the various industries leaving an area or moving into an area. Tap into these excellent sources of information.

ORGANIZE TO ANALYZE

Now that you've gathered a lot of information, you need to organize it in order to analyze it well so you can do your negotiation plan (see Chapter 3). By writing this plan, you create your own customized tools to keep track of properties and their particular data, strengths, and weaknesses.

The sample chart in Figure 2.8 will help you assess a property prior to and during a negotiation process. Charts like this can be valuable reference tools, especially when you are negotiating parallel deals and need a "picture" to refer to quickly.

From here, let's go on to create your negotiation plan.

SUMMARY POINTS FOR CHAPTER 2: THE IMPORTANCE OF BEING PREPARED

- Gathering information is not enough; it is essential that you validate the information that you have obtained.
- The skilled, experienced negotiator will accrue ten hours in preparation time to get ready for a one-hour negotiation session.
- By documenting each step of the negotiation process, you improve the negotiation itself and gain negotiating strength at the same time.

FIGURE 2.8 *Product Accessment Information*

Investment Property, West 17th Street		
Asking price	$4,900,000	
Office square feet	22,500	
Retail square feet	2,500	
Basement	2,500	
Total square feet	27,500	
Price/square foot	$ 178.18	
Percent leased	100%	
Floors	10	
Class	C	
Gross income	$466,729.00	not verified
Expenses	$141,187.00	not verified
Net operating income	$325,542.00	
Current asking rent/ square foot	$24.00	

Negative factors
- Building has structural concerns
- 4 rent-stabilized tenants

Positive factors
- 25' wide
- Unused development rights
- Space will be delivered vacant

Recommended strategy to add value
- Use the need to fix the structural problem as a way to relocate the IMD tenants
- Increase office rents to $24/square foot
- Increase retail rents to $55/square foot
- Reduce expenses by 5%

Investment Property, West 17th Street			
Total gross income	$470,000	to	$677,500
Expenses from	$141,187	to	$134,128
Net operating income from	$328,813	to	$543,372

Using various cap rates, the new value is computed:

	6%	7%	8%
New value	$9,056,206	$7,762,462	$6,792,154
Strike price	4,655,000	4,655,000	4,655,000
(5% asking)			
Profit	$4,401,206	$3,107,462	$2,137,154

Source: © George F. Donohue

- Having thorough, clearly written, dated material from your nego-tiation sessions gives you a powerful advantage in the event you find yourself in litigation.
- Lead your opponent into a discussion where you can declare an indisputable. It will give you the same powerful feeling as declaring "checkmate" at the end of a chess match.

3

YOUR
NEGOTIATION PLAN

Good hitters don't just go up and swing. They always have a plan. Call it an educated
deduction. You visualize. You're like a good negotiator. You know what you have,
you know what he has, then you try to work it out.

Dave Winfield

The success of the negotiation depends on your plan, which I refer to as your Negotiation Dossier. "Dossier" is originally a French word meaning a bundle of documents labeled on the back (in French, "dos" means the back). This word also stems from the Latin "dorsum," which means back as well.

Dossiers are filled with detailed records on a particular person and/or subject and important items to carry out an assignment. In Ian Fleming's novels, for example, James Bond is always handed a dossier before any important assignment.

Similarly, you need to create your "dossier" before carrying out each of your assignments. The dossier brings together all the materials and information that relate to the potential strengths, weaknesses, and goals of the negotiation plan. It creates a systematic approach to reflect on the plan and makes sure all components of each negotiation are covered. Keeping everything in one organized place enables you to find facts quickly—which is important if you need to strike while the iron is hot on a real estate deal.

The following dossier template can be modified and adapted to your specific transactions. Please note that in some sections of the negotiation dossier, you will see the word "attach" in parentheses. When you see "attach," be sure to include the appropriate information in your dossier to make it complete.

Negotiation Dossier for 100 Main Street

I. **General Information** (see Chapter 2)
Investment goal: _____
Property address: _____
Asking price: _____
Square footage: _____
Number of floors: _____
Year built: _____
Zoning: _____
Number of tenants: _____
Gross income: $ _____
(attach setup)
Expenses: $ _____
(attach validation, bills, etc.)
Net operating income: $_____

Valuation (see Chapter 9)
Income approach $ _____
(attach calculation)
Market approach $ _____
(attach comparables)
Replacement approach $ _____
(attach calculation)
How shall the price be characterized:
_____ Price per building
_____ Price per floor
_____ Price per square foot
_____ Other

Repairs required:
1. _____ ($_____)
2. _____ ($_____)

3. _____ ($_____)
4. _____ ($_____)
5. _____ ($_____)

_____ Complete (Move to Section II.)

II.   **Market Information** (see Chapter 2)
      Review all that apply to this transaction:
      _____ Trends in home sales
      _____ Interest rates
      _____ Consumer price index
      _____ Unemployment rate
      _____ Vacancy rate
      _____ Absorption rate
      _____ Fastest-growing businesses
      _____ Any new laws that can affect this transaction
      _____ Other _____
      _____ Other _____

      _____ Complete (Move to Section III.)

III. **Partners (if applicable)** (see Chapter 5)
      Discuss and agree to:
      _____ The goal of the investment
      _____ Investment amounts
      _____ Budgets
      _____ Strategy, if more money is required during ownership
      _____ Responsibilities
      _____ Exit strategy
      _____ Tax structure
      _____ Ownership structure
      _____ Sign partners agreement (attach agreement)
      _____ Complete (Move to Section IV.)

IV.   **Financing/Bankers** (see Chapter 6)
      _____ Create and review banker matrix (attach)
      _____ Conduct financing research (attach)
      _____ Prepare personal financial statement (attach)
      _____ Create the income approach analysis (attach)

_____ Visit the "dress rehearsal" bank

_____ Choose financing source

Name of bank: _____

Loan officer: _____

Address: _____

Office telephone: _____

Cell number: _____

Fax: _____

E-mail: _____

_____ Obtain preapproval letter (attach)

_____ Prepare agenda for negotiation meeting (attach)

_____ Select and agree to place to hold negotiation

_____ Complete (Move to Section V.)

V. Real Estate Brokers (see Chapter 7)

_____ Interview at least three real estate brokers

Name: _____

Address: _____

Office telephone: _____

Cell number: _____

Fax: _____

E-mail: _____

Name: _____

Address: _____

Office telephone: _____

Cell number: _____

Fax: _____

E-mail: _____

Name: _____

Address: _____

Office telephone: _____

Cell number: _____

Fax: _____

E-mail: _____

_____ Prepare agenda for negotiation meeting (attach)

_____ Select and agree on place to hold negotiation

_____ Sign real estate brokerage agreement (attach)

  _____ Term of agreement

  _____ Commission fee

  _____ Who pays the commission?

  _____ Escape clause

  _____ Broker's responsibilities

_____ Complete (Move to Section VI.)

VI. **Lawyers** (see Chapter 8)

_____ Interview at least three lawyers

Name: _____

Address: _____

Office telephone: _____

Cell number: _____

Fax: _____

E-mail: _____

Name: _____

Address: _____

Office telephone: _____

Cell number: _____

Fax: _____

E-mail: _____

Name: _____

Address: _____

Office telephone: _____

Cell number: _____

Fax: _____

E-mail: 74 _____

_____ Create the lawyer matrix

_____ Prepare agenda for negotiation meeting (attach)

_____ Select and agree on place to hold negotiation

_____ Sign an agreement with lawyer (attach)

      _____ Flat fee

      _____ Out-of-pocket expenses

      _____ Capping the fee

      _____ Retainer

      _____ Payment schedule

      _____ Lawyer's responsibilities

      _____ Transaction time line

_____ Complete (Move to Section VII.)

VII. Seller (see Chapter 9)

Name: _____

Address: _____

Office telephone: _____

Cell number: _____

Fax: _____

E-mail: _____

Determine the reason for the sale:

Reason: _____

Reason supplied by: _____

Is the seller under any deadline? _____

Seller profile:

      Age: _____

      Marital status: _____

      Occupation: _____

      Personality: _____

Create the seller matrix:

      The seller's triangle: _____

      Your triangle: _____

      The combined elements: _____

_____ Create the five-column matrix (attach)

_____ Who has signature authority? _____

_____ Interview with neighbor

Seller's weaknesses:

1. _____
2. _____
3. _____
4. _____
5. _____

Seller's strengths:

1. _____
2. _____
3. _____
4. _____
5. _____

My weaknesses:

1. _____
2. _____
3. _____
4. _____
5. _____

My strengths:

1. _____
2. _____
3. _____
4. _____
5. _____

List of "indisputables" I can state: (see Chapter 2)

1. _____
2. _____
3. _____
4. _____
5. _____

_____ Prepare agenda for negotiation meeting (attach) (see Chapter 13)

_____ Select and agree on place to hold negotiation

_____ Complete (Move to Section VIII.)

VIII. Contractors (if applicable) (see Chapter 10)
_____ Interview at least three contractors

Name: _____

Address: _____

Office telephone: _____

Cell number: _____

Fax: _____

E-mail: _____

Name: _____

Address: _____

Office telephone: _____

Cell number: _____

Fax: _____

E-mail: _____

Name: _____

Address: _____

Office telephone: _____

Cell number: _____

Fax: _____

E-mail: _____

_____ Obtain inspector's opinion on repairs

_____ Penalty and reward clauses

_____ Up-front fees

_____ Payment schedule

_____ Project duration

_____ Prepare agenda for negotiation meeting (attach)

_____ Select and agree on place on hold negotiation

_____ Sign an agreement with contractor (attach)

_____ Complete (Move to Section IX.)

IX.   Property Managers (see Chapter 11)
_____ Interview at least three property managers

Name: _____

Address: _____

Office telephone: _____

Cell number: _____

Fax: _____

E-mail: _____

Name: _____

Address: _____

Office telephone: _____

Cell number: _____

Fax: _____

E-mail: _____

Name: _____

Address: _____

Office telephone: _____

Cell number: _____

Fax: _____

E-mail: _____

_____ Fee

_____ Duration of contract

_____ Responsibilities

_____ Escape clause

_____ Prepare agenda for negotiation meeting (attach)

_____ Select and agree on place on hold negotiation

_____ Sign an agreement with property manager (attach)

_____ Complete (Move to Section X.)

X. Tenants (see Chapter 12)

Commercial tenants:

_____ Obtain financial statements (attach)

_____ Obtain tax ID number

_____ Review tenant's Web site

_____ Obtain credit check

_____ Prepare agenda for negotiation meeting (attach)

_____ Select and agree on place to hold negotiation

_____ Negotiate lease term sheet: (attach)

     _____ Base rate

     _____ Term of lease

     _____ Lease commencement

     _____ Rent commencement

     _____ Operating escalations

     _____ Real estate tax

     _____ Security deposit

     _____ Construction work

     _____ Subleasing and assignment

     _____ Restoration clause

     _____ Other clauses _____

_____ Complete (Move to Section XI.)

XI.   Ethical Self-Evaluation (see Chapter 14)

This section is added to give you a moment of reflection in regarding your ethical behavior in your transaction.

     _____ Have you negotiated in good faith?

     _____ Regarding the legal documents, is everything you supplied accurate and truthful?

     _____ From an ethical point of view, is there anything you have done in this negotiation that is bothering you?

     _____ If so, can it be straightened out?

     _____ Have you fulfilled the obligations that you have committed to?

     _____ Has anyone who represented you acted unethically?

     _____ Have you compromised your values?

_____ Complete (Move to Section XII.)

XII.   Role-Playing (see Chapter 15)

     _____ Scenario One, enacted on (enter date): _____

Performance rated as:

     _____ Excellent

     _____ Good

     _____ Fair

     _____ Poor

_____ Scenario Two, enacted on (enter date): _____
Performance rated as:

     _____ Excellent

     _____ Good

     _____ Fair

     _____ Poor

_____ Scenario Three, enacted on (enter date):_____
Performance rated as:

     _____ Excellent

     _____ Good

     _____ Fair

     _____ Poor

_____ Complete (Move to Section XIII.)

XIII. Appendix

Also included in this dossier should be:

     _____ All correspondence

     _____ All offers and counteroffers

Source: © George F. Donohue

4

FUNDAMENTALS OF A NEGOTIATION

Firmness in support of fundamentals, with flexibility in tactics and methods,

is the key to any hope of progress in negotiation.

Dwight D. Eisenhower

What exactly is negotiating? *It's an exchange of information and ideas with the purpose of reaching a decision that's mutually accepted by all parties involved.*

When teaching the principles of negotiation to thousands of people, I do this exercise: At the beginning of each class, I distribute a piece of paper that has one sentence with two blanks. It states: "I intend to negotiate for _____, and my biggest fear is _____."
I ask the students to think carefully before writing their answers. Even though it's a simple statement, it often takes people a long time to fill in the blanks. The classes I have taught have been comprised of many different types of people from all walks of life, age groups, and backgrounds. Still, I have found that their answers are quite similar.

For the first blank, most people write "a new home." For the second blank, the predominant answers are:

- I'm not going to get the best price.
- I will be taken advantage of.
- I will sound foolish.
- I will not know what to do.

These common concerns and fears are completely normal for people who haven't gained a lot of experience in negotiating. By the time you've read this book and employed these ideas, I think you'll find these fears will have much less power over you.

WHO BLINKS FIRST?

A controversial question among professional negotiators is: "Who should send in the first offer?" Some experienced negotiators believe showing your opening hand first is a sign of weakness. However, I'm not concerned as much with *who* should send the first offer as with *how* the opening bid should be played.

It's interesting to note that the first offer is sometimes referred to as the opening salvo. The word "salvo" has a few meanings. The first is what most people think of: a discharge of artillery; a volley with artillery or firearms. It also means an outburst of applause, which is a sign of respect and appreciation.

If you're in a position of strength and are dealing with an astute opponent—and you feel confident there is more than one opponent you can choose to negotiate with—it may be more effective for you to open the bid. Do so with conviction, clarity, and confidence.

The Tree with Two Branches

I've had the pleasure of traveling to several traditional towns as well as modern cities in China. They include places such as Xian, Tianjin, Shanghai, and Beijing. In one city, I became friendly with an old Chinese gentleman and discussed negotiations with him.

He told a story with indelible imagery that I always conjure up in my mind when I hear the phrase "flexibility in negotiations." The old man said: "There existed two branches on two different trees that were standing alongside each other in the forest. It began to snow heavily. The snowflakes fell in a chaotic manner, pummeling the forest.

"One branch stood rigid and firm. The snow gathered quickly, piling ever so high on the branch until, due to the branch's resistance, it snapped and fell to the ground. The second branch, which remained flexible, bent every so often, allowing some of the snow to be shed from its limb. This branch survived the storm and grew stronger from the experience."

This concept of flexibility is not uniquely Chinese. I believe it is a universal tenet that must be understood and employed judiciously when negotiating. Having a plan is paramount; being flexible throughout the execution of the plan will work to your advantage. You will be the "branch" that survives.

MOTIVATION IS THE LOCOMOTIVE

I think negotiators can be compared to trains moving along one track on a network of rails. These trains have the ability to go as slow or as fast as the engineers desire, and they will have the opportunity to choose various routes to get to their destinations. Motivation provides the energy in negotiation, like a locomotive moves a train.

What motivates the person on the other side of your negotiation table? Well, it depends on the various characters involved in your real estate transaction. Each of them has a different motivating force that brings them across from you at the negotiation table.

Money could be the motivator. So could pride, prestige, and even the satisfaction of doing a good job. It's important to analyze the person and be cognizant at all times of the "locomotive" in each of them. That locomotion of motivation is heading straight toward you.

Not Always Motivated by Price

Contrary to popular belief, your opponents' motivation won't always be price. In fact, two factors are present in every negotiation: speed and price. Some people need to move money quickly, which motivates them to unload property right away. In this case, understanding speed/momentum can be more important than determining the best pricing.

How can you test the importance of speed to your opponents? I suggest you try to nail down the closing date up front. For example, say, "I've got to close in 30 days" and watch their reactions. Are they okay with that requirement? Do they even *want* to nail down the closing date? If not, it becomes your clue that an issue is lingering and needs to be discussed. If they don't give a specific date or they ask for 90 to 120 days to close, it could mean they might be "shopping" your deal.

Be leery of those who want a long period to close the deal. Don't hesitate to find out why. Remember, if it's a good deal but has a long closing period, that factor can work against you because another party might come in and offer them more for the property. Or they might intend to flip or assign the contract. At the closing, they might even bring in others who are buying it from them. Or, in 120 days, the market might go up and the value of a $170,000 property might rise to $200,000.

Do you see the various ways a long closing can work against you? I suggest you do your best to find out the truth about their situation as early in the process as you can.

UNDERSTAND PERSONALITIES AND MOODS

Personality traits and moods also can affect the actions of your opponents. During the negotiation, especially in the beginning, take the "temperature" of your opponents because it will affect their negotiation style. Observe their emotional states: Are they nervous, relaxed, angry, bitter, or confident? What else is going on with them? Ask them lots of questions.

It's possible that you might have to deal with someone who doesn't appear to have a stable state of mind. Be sure to investigate the reason for his or her behavior. Certainly don't ignore it, but rather, the best way to handle emotional instability is by asking a direct question. For example, you might ask, "Is there something else outside the negotiation that's bothering you? Perhaps we should continue this discussion another time."

I've heard amazing responses when I've suggested postponing the discussion. Sometimes the answer brings up an opportunity to bond with the person. He or she may say something like, "I just had a disagreement this morning with my son about going to college. It seems he would rather join a rock-and-roll band." That's good information, and it may provide an opening for you to talk about your children and similar incidents that have occurred in your family. The bonus is that you create rapport while helping that person get focused on the discussion at hand.

If the person is obviously angry or bitter and offers no explanation, postpone the negotiation session if you possibly can. Certainly you could both regret the results if you continue.

Similarly, people who seem overly confident in their actions or words could have a strong advantage over you. Perhaps they're even running parallel transactions with your competitors. In these situations, be careful of moving too fast or giving ultimatums. It's almost always better to reschedule, so be open to that possibility.

BE A DETECTIVE

Skilled negotiators have enhanced their powers of observation. Be sure to hone yours! If you are negotiating at the other party's office or home, look around like you're a detective. Observe as much detail as possible without appearing to be distracted or aloof. For example, if you see that your opponent has a great many nautical-themed objects in his office, strike up a conversation about boating or sailing. Or perhaps you notice some photographs of children. Having an interesting exchange about your opponent's children or grandchildren can be a great ice-breaker before you dive in to the negotiation itself.

Remember, negotiating is about *people,* not about property. Therefore, it's important to understand people: how they act and react. Their surroundings give you clues about their values and interests. Take time to notice if your opponent's desk displays family photos . . . or not. Notice if the environment itself is neat or messy. Always pay attention to how your opponents behave in their own spaces, and use the information you glean to understand more about them.

For example, if you see lots of photos and symbols of respect, you can assume they act above board and aren't totally business-oriented. If they appear to be neat, you can assume the negotiation will go smoothly, be precise, and be run on time rather than become a drawn-out, touchy-feely experience.

If, on the other hand, you see a lot of mess, then you can predict that the negotiation will be freewheeling and disorganized. As a result, you'll have to be more on the ball and stay on top of the discussions. Most important, don't lose sight of the reason you're meeting across the table, and stay focused on reaching a mutually acceptable conclusion.

WATCH FOR BIAS

Not being aware of your own biases can definitely hurt your negotiation. Research has shown that when two teams participate in a negotiation, each team automatically holds biased views about the opposing team. They frequently believe that members of the other team are

- not as smart as they are, or
- not as honest or moral as they are.

Don't let biases like these cloud your perception of those on the other side of the table. Negotiate as though that team matches yours equally. This is another reason it's important to do extensive research about the other side's capabilities beforehand. Know who your opponents are!

WHAT DO WE NEGOTIATE FIRST?

In a real estate negotiation and in other similar acts of mediation, the lead negotiator determines where to start. Consider these options:

- Do you begin in a headstrong way and tackle the most contentious element of the transaction first?
- Do you save all the elements that seem too tough to compromise on until the end of the negotiation session?
- Do you start at a random place, with no forethought?
- Do you let your opponents begin with the topics they want to tackle instead of speaking up about yours first?

The answer to all these questions is a resounding "No." You need to gather as much information as you can and then formulate the sequence of your plan. That plan should begin with ranking the priorities of each party. Of course, priorities vary from person to person, but most likely they will encompass items such as the following:

- Pricing
- Timing of the transaction
- Financing
- Fees and who pays them

- Contingencies
- Legal matters
- Repairs and construction matters
- Responsibilities of each party

Getting a Grasp on the Process

"A bad process can kill a good man!" I made this statement often when I managed the leasing of the World Trade Center in the 1990s. To me, this statement shows the importance of having a grasp on the process before you begin any negotiation.

Be sure you understand each step of the negotiation process. Think through the process. Create your negotiation dossier (see Chapter 3), which means *write down* your negotiation plan. Above all, don't let the unknowns of the process kill your deal.

KEEP GAUGING, NOT GOUGING

Ranking the negotiation's elements in order of importance helps you determine which aspects of the deal will be least confrontational. I believe it's important to begin the negotiations with noncontroversial elements. This helps you gauge the negotiating power of the other party and it creates a mutual ground on which to build the negotiation itself.

The following figures will help you uncover the components of the deal that you need to tackle first. The first few figures illustrate how one negotiator evaluated the other party's position and how he decided to choose the opening topics.

The information this negotiator used to gauge the opponent was collected from three sources:

1. Informal direct conversations over the phone with the seller
2. Information from the one inspection he went on with the real estate broker
3. A few brief conversations with the seller's neighbors

When referring to these figures, keep in mind that you should choose at least six components of the deal to examine. Fill in the box at the top of each pyramid with the component that is most important to you. Fill in the bottom box with elements that have a lower consequence to you, but are still part of the deal.

SCENARIO ONE

In the first scenario, the down payment is your primary concern. You have limited funds and will pay a little more than the asking price if you can keep within your down payment budget.

You've learned from your detective work that the owner of the property is firm on the price being asked and has turned down a few other offers. You recognize that the house has *personalty*—which includes beautiful furniture, paintings, antiques, a washer and dryer, and so on—that you are interested in buying. Clearly, having these extras would make moving into the property more convenient for you. The seller also recognizes that the house's personalty has value in the sale.

Figure 4.1 illustrates the buyer's ranking of the elements of the deal. Having a low down payment is the most important item to the buyer in this example.

FIGURE 4.1 *Buyer's Ranking of Deal*

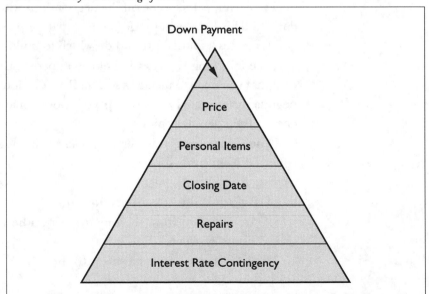

Source: © George F. Donohue

FIGURE 4.2 *Seller's Ranking of Deal*

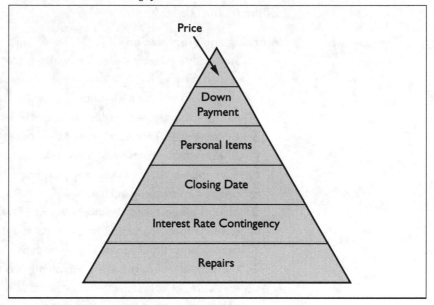

Source: © George F. Donohue

Figure 4.2 illustrates the seller's ranking of what is most important to him in this transaction. Obtaining a high price ranks at the top for this seller.

Figure 4.3 blends the buyer's rankings and the seller's rankings to help determine the points least likely to be contentious and to provide a "road map" to get through various waypoints of the negotiation.

FIGURE 4.3 *Blend of Buyer and Seller's Rankings*

BUYER	SELLER
Down payment	Price
Price	Down payment
Personal items	Personal items
Closing date	Closing date
Repairs	Interest rate contingency
Interest rate contingency	Repairs

Source: © George F. Donohue

Come to the Table!

Working the Negotiation

1. *Start with the lowest-ranked common element.* The diagram tells you to start with the "closing date" issue because it's the lowest-ranked common element. Focus the opening subjects on having a short due diligence and a quick decision about setting a closing date. Therefore, one of the opening remarks could be: "If everything represented here today can be validated by both of us and we can reach an acceptable price, I would like to agree on the closing to be held within 30 days."

2. *Move to the next similarly ranked element.* In this situation, the next element to tackle would be personal items, which is the only other element ranked similarly by both parties. The next step of the negotiation might begin something like this: "The personal items are, of course, very minor compared to the actual property itself. I would like to recommend that we throw them into the deal." Keep in mind that I have only cited a couple of sentences to begin the dialogue. In reality, the discussion on both the closing date and the personalty will be much longer. It's during these discussions that you will be able to discern the negotiation skills and sense of "reasonableness" of the other party.

3. *Reaching a fork in the road:*

   - *Seller is not reasonable—get the seller to concede.* If you're the buyer and the seller is playing hardball, your goal will be to get the seller to concede to what you want on your most important issue—the amount of the down payment. You would say something like this: "I recognize that the personalty and closing date are important to you. One critical element I need before going forward with you on this deal is my being able to put down 10 percent toward the purchase price." If the seller accepts this arrangement, then you can move to the price issue and try to lock in an agreement on the number.

   - *Seller is reasonable—go for more.* On the other hand, if you find that during the personal items and closing date discussion your opponent has been reasonable, you may wish to go down in the ranking to see if you can get the buyer to pay for repairs and give you an interest rate contingency. You may be able to obtain these elements of the deal, knowing they're not that important to the seller.

4. *Finish the negotiation.* The last elements (repairs and the interest rate contingency) should then be easy to negotiate through because they weren't of paramount importance to either of you.

Now that you know where you stand on all of the issues, move to discussing a low down payment. If you find the seller resisting to accept a low down payment position, you can give back one or more of the other subordinate things to achieve your most important goal.

SCENARIO TWO

In this second scenario, the negotiation is between the owner of the building and a prospective tenant. As the owner of the building, you have had an informal conversation with the prospective tenant and have learned that the occupancy date is not a critical issue. You also realize you have a bit of flexibility regarding the occupancy date.

Keep in mind that you construct these diagrams based on your best educated guesses about what is important to your opponent. The following scenario shows how to sequence the issues that you'll negotiate. Slight variations in the sequence may result in the same final outcome. It's important to determine the best *sequence* so you can develop a plan of action.

Figure 4.4 shows the prospective tenant's ranking of the elements required to complete a potential lease transaction. It indicates that obtaining a low rental rate is the most important element for this person.

Figure 4.5 illustrates the landlord's ranking of what is most important in this potential lease transaction. The landlord wants to obtain a rent that is equal to or greater than the market rent.

Figure 4.6 blends the buyer's rankings and the seller's rankings to help determine the points least likely to be contentious and to provide a "road map" to get through the waypoints of the negotiation.

FIGURE 4.4 *Tenant's Ranking of Deal*

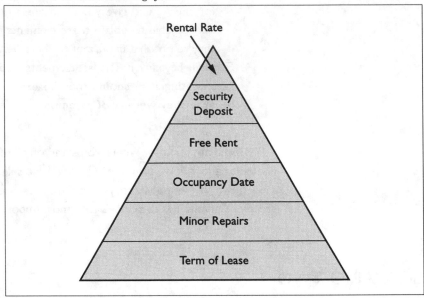

Source: © George F. Donohue

FIGURE 4.5 *Landlord's Ranking of Deal*

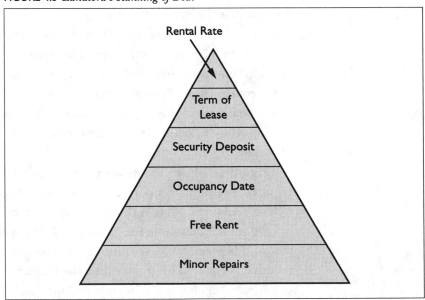

Source: © George F. Donohue

FIGURE 4.6 *Blend of Tenant and Landlord's Rankings of Deal*

TENANT	LANDLORD
Rental rate—low	Rental rate—high
Security deposit	Term of lease
Free rent	Security deposit
Occupancy date	Occupancy date
Minor repairs	Free rent
Term of lease	Minor repairs

Source: © George F. Donohue

Come to the Table!

Working the Negotiation

1. *Start with the lowest-ranked common element.* Figure 4.6 illustrates that the lowest-ranked common element is the occupancy date. The opening dialogue should focus on the schedule, beginning this way: "Well, it appears that we are both flexible on the occupancy date. I suggest we choose June 1 as the occupancy date and make it subject to postponement."

2. *Move to the next similarly ranked element.* In this scenario, the next similarly ranked element is a little less clear than in the first scenario. As the building owner, you next want to address the "minor repairs" because this is inconsequential to you in this particular transaction. Find something of value that you are providing the tenant and demonstrate good-faith negotiations early in the process.

3. *Reaching a fork in the road.* At this point, it might be prudent to tackle the issue of the lease term. Because it is an important item to you and you have already demonstrated good-faith negotiating, you'll likely be able to obtain the term that you desire.

   The next item would be the free rent. Similar to the minor repairs, it is something that you want to stress you are giving to the tenant, even though it isn't that important to you in this particular transaction.

4. *Finishing the negotiation.* The final stretch in this negotiation would be to negotiate the security deposit, and then seek to obtain the highest rent possible. If the tenant resists paying a higher rent, then explain that if the tenant can't pay the rent rate you are seeking, some of the other elements provided will need to be adjusted. For example, if in the negotiation your conjecture about the importance of the free rent and the security deposit was correct, you'd counter by saying, "If that's the highest rent you are offering, then the free rent has to be reduced dramatically—or to nothing. In addition, I insist that the security deposit be twice the amount and that I will not be able to do the minor repairs."

The negotiation will then take a turn. If the tenant comes up in the amount of rent he or she is willing to pay to gain some other components, you will either successfully close the deal or be close to closing it.

Alternatively, it could go in another direction. The tenant could resist coming up to the rental rate that you've requested. That means you may have to walk away from the negotiation to demonstrate how important it is for you to obtain a particular amount.

LYING: THE MENDACITY WE LIVE WITH

One of the most difficult, frustrating aspects of negotiation is dealing with people who tell lies. Although certain critics would say that negotiation is all about lies, recognize that there's a big difference between those who posture and position themselves by withholding information, compared to those who deliberately and maliciously lie during the negotiation.

People in general are more practiced at *deceiving* one another than they are at *detecting* lies. Okay. I prefer not to dance around the issue. Let me just say that people lie. I have seen firsthand the frustration and damage caused by a liar's duplicity. In particular, I empathize with the young real estate brokers and investors who have lost deals because someone completely and intentionally deceived them.

WHY PEOPLE USE DECEPTION

You'll meet many characters doing real estate negotiations. To guard yourself against being duped by a liar, it's critical to gain an understanding of how and why people use deception. Since the tragic events of September 11, 2001, and the creation of the Homeland Security Department in the United States, there has been an increase in the number of research studies conducted by the U.S. Government and private companies on the subject of lying (from a report by the Consortium of Social Sciences Associations who focused its first Congressional Briefing of 2004 on the topic of Detecting Deception: Research to Secure the Homeland).

Let's examine some interesting facts about deception and how to detect it. Many people assume the number one way to tell if people lie is if they turn away their eyes while speaking. This is a false perception. Those who study liars say they don't change their gaze or touch their nose or clear their throats any more than people who are telling the truth. But it's possible to identify a number of telltale signs people display when they're not telling the truth. These signs are:

- They move their arms and hands less than normal.
- They blink fewer times than normal.
- Their voices can become more high-pitched than normal.
- They make fewer speech errors than normal.
- They pause longer while speaking than normal.
- They're more likely to lie during phone calls than during face-to-face meetings.
- They use the same phrase to answer a question that has been repeated to them.
- They respond to others who show suspicion with increased embellishment.
- Their pupil size increases and their lips press but they don't necessarily blink or change their posture.

Rachel Adelson, in the American Psychological Association's online magazine (Volume 35, No. 7, July/August 2004), reports findings from a recent, unpublished meta-analysis of 253 studies of people distinguishing truths from lies. They revealed overall accuracy was just 53 percent—

not much better than flipping a coin. That means that in experiments in which a listener was told a number of true and false statements and the listener's goal was to determine when the person was lying, the listener had trouble detecting the lies. The average listener could only guess correctly 53 percent of the time.

Become aware of the parallels between these findings and real estate negotiating to determine if someone is being deceptive. To protect yourself from being deceived in real estate negotiations, pay close attention to both the verbal and nonverbal cues discussed here. Make a point of enhancing your ability to detect deception through practice and training.

Being **R**eady to **W**alk **A**way

Quite often, you might hear someone say, "I'm going to walk away from the deal." But it's a major action to actually walk out on a negotiation. If properly orchestrated, making this statement can be an effective tool in negotiating. I believe that it's rare in real estate negotiations, but it's still important to address the subject of walking away from a deal.

To explain the effectiveness of doing a "walkout," here is an actual experience I had: I was working at the Teleport office park, which at the time was a state-of-the-art 100-acre office park in New York City. As part of my job, I would solicit tenants and developers to build and/or lease space at the office park. It also included assisting in lease negotiations.

In one particular incident, we were negotiating with a major international construction company that was developing $5 billion worth of real estate in various parts of the world. The principals had shown interest in building in our office park, but had been dragging the negotiation on and on.

At that time, my boss Robert had at least 20 more years of experience in negotiations than I did. A keen planner and savvy negotiator, Robert requested a session at this developer's conference room and asked me to join him. I thought it was odd that he set it up to go to *their* conference room, especially because of their obstinate position at this point in the negotiation. Quite frankly, I thought holding the meeting on their turf showed a sign of weakness on our part. Little did I know what Robert had in store for our opponents.

We arrived on time with our agenda and we began the discussions. After approximately an hour of negotiation, we had achieved little progress. Robert asked the four men sitting across from us if they needed time to confer privately. They thanked him for the suggestion and politely left the room to strategize. As soon as they closed the door, Robert turned to me and stated confidently, "Get up, we're leaving." I was stunned. But I didn't ask any questions. I got up, followed him at a fast pace out of the conference room, down the hall, into the elevator, and out of the building.

Once we hit the pavement of Manhattan, I asked Robert if he'd lost his mind. After all, it's hard to come by prospective clients like this developer we'd just walked away from. He told me not to worry and we went back to his office. Once we arrived there, I asked him, "Now what?"

In the next few chapters, you'll meet the cast of characters you'll do business with in the course of a typical real estate negotiation. Typically, you'll interact with at least eight different types of people along the way. They are:

1. Partners
2. Bankers
3. Real estate brokers
4. Lawyers
5. Sellers
6. General contractors
7. Property managers
8. Buyers

Each character has a specific motivation and goal relative to the transaction you're trying to close and depending on if he or she is on your team or on your opponent's team. Because of their professions, some may have a higher negotiating aptitude and a lot more experience than you. Be forewarned: Not all negotiating tactics work on all types of people, so pay attention and keep learning.

SUMMARY POINTS FOR CHAPTER 4: FUNDAMENTALS OF A NEGOTIATION

- Employ these ideas and fear will have much less power over you.
- Having a plan is paramount; being flexible throughout the execution of the plan will work to your advantage.
- Skilled negotiators have enhanced their powers of observation. Be sure to hone yours!
- Don't be concerned as much with who should send the first offer as with how the opening bid should be played.
- Rank the elements you and your opponent care about the most in the negotiations and determine their best sequence so you can develop a plan of action.
- Liars don't change their gaze or touch their nose or clear their throat any more often than people who are telling the truth. But you can identify a number of telltale signs people display when they're lying.

5

PARTNERS—THE OTHER HALF OF YOU

He who draws only on his own resources easily comes to an end of his wealth.

William Hazlitt

It may be necessary for you to have a partner when purchasing a property, which makes this individual the first person to negotiate with. Especially because this person will be your partner, be sure your negotiation sessions are open, frank, and transparent. And, as I always stress, memorialize or document every piece of your negotiation in writing. This could save both of you a great deal of heartache and even possible litigation in the future.

POINTS OF PARTNERSHIP NEGOTIATIONS

The following are the most important points to consider when negotiating with someone who might become your partner:

- *Initial investment.* What is the amount of money each partner will put into this investment?
- *Common goal of the investment.* What will buying this property produce for the partners?

- *Budget setting.* How much will be needed for repairs and other costs?
- *Additional capital.* What will you do if more money is required?
- *Distribution of responsibility.* What does each partner do to manage the property?
- *Exit strategy.* When will you sell?
- *Tax structure.* How does it need to be different for each partner?
- *Ownership structure.* What form of organizational structure will you put in place?

Initial Investment

One of the key aspects of a partnership is how much money each person will invest. Ideally, each partner invests equal amounts—that's less problematic than investing different amounts. But sometimes partners don't have equal amounts of capital to invest. Especially if one person wants to put in hard cash and the other "sweat equity" (physical labor), it's critical to define each partner's responsibilities in full.

Common Goal of the Investment

Some people are "patient" money investors; they have time to wait. So they want to keep a building for ten years and then sell. Others operate from a "flipping" strategy. To flippers (people who buy and sell the same property quickly), two years is a long time to hold a piece of property. I suggest you determine your common goal up front as you negotiate a minimum term that's acceptable to all the partners.

Budget Setting

In addition to the initial investment dollars, you'll require money to fix up the property and carry out minor monthly repairs, so be sure to negotiate a maximum amount to allocate for these additional expenses. Most important, decide who will kick in this money when it's required—now and in the future.

Additional Capital

In the event that more money is required than you first estimated, be sure to negotiate into the agreement the maximum amount that each party will be required to kick in. Also define under what circumstances each investor will be required to invest more money.

Distribution of Responsibility

You'll find that some partners are just better at certain management responsibilities of owning real estate than others. For example, the responsibilities could be distributed as follows:

- John Smith will manage all *physical* aspects of owning the property including repairs to both the inside of the apartments and to the exterior of the building. These responsibilities may cover routine maintenance, snow removal, hallway lights, boiler upkeep, and so on.
- Michael Jones will manage all *accounting* aspects of owning the property. This will include producing monthly reports on the income and expenses related to the building, collecting the rents, paying the appropriate vendors and bills, filing the income tax, and so on.
- David Richardson will manage all *tenant relations*. This will include advertising, interviewing tenants, issuing leases, conducting credit and background checks, monitoring lease expirations, and related activities.

Of course, depending on your relationship with your partners, the list of responsibilities can be more detailed or more general. This example provides you with the spirit of how the responsibilities could be distributed.

Exit Strategy

Your exit strategy lays out the agreed-on circumstances under which one or more of the parties can exit the partnership. For example, you may want to negotiate and predetermine the following:

The building will be sold if: a) three years have passed since it was purchased, or b) the value of the property is 150 percent of its original value. (For example, the property was bought for $200,000 and an appraiser has determined it's now worth $300,000, so now is the time to sell, as agreed on.)

Also negotiate an exit strategy in case only one of the partners wants to exit the investment. Start by hiring an appraiser to determine the value of the property. Generally, the partner who wants to exit early pays half of the difference between the existing mortgage and the appraised value of the investment property.

Tax Structure

If there are two or more partners involved in an investment, their tax situations will most likely be different from each other, therefore the future tax planning for the property also would be different for each partner. Have your accountant advise you on the best tax structure so you can negotiate this into the agreement.

Ownership Structure

I'm often asked what type of ownership structure is best for buying property. The answer is, "It depends." In making a choice, you will want to take into account the following:

- Your vision regarding the size and nature of your business.
- The level of control you wish to have.
- The level of "structure" you are willing to deal with.
- The business's vulnerability to lawsuits.
- The tax implications of the different ownership structures.
- The expected profit (or loss) of the business.
- Whether or not you need to reinvest earnings into the business.
- Your need to take cash out of the business for yourself.

Your choices include:

- Sole proprietorship
- Partnership

- Corporation
- Subchapter S corporation
- Limited liability company (LLC)

Deciding how to structure your real estate business has long-term implications, so I suggest getting advice from your accountant and attorney before selecting a form of ownership structure. Refer to Appendix A for descriptions of the choices noted above, as defined by the U.S. Small Business Administration (http://www.sba.org). This appendix also includes a list of the appropriate government forms required for each.

Partnership Pitfalls and Benefits

When buying property with partners, especially with people you know, it's important to take a thorough approach. Minimally, you would cover all points cited above and perhaps add unique categories that are important to you and your partners. You've likely heard too many horror stories about people losing their friendships, marriages, or life savings over a business deal that was poorly put together. The root of these mishaps comes from poor negotiations or no negotiations at all.

The best partnerships are composed of people who are proficient in different disciplines. Ideally, a general contractor, lawyer, and accountant would form a good partnership regarding the buying, managing, and selling of real estate property. Here's how: The general contractor would provide discounted labor and materials for repairs and improvements. The lawyer could handle contract of sale, leases, and any other legal matter. The accountant would closely monitor all of the operating expenses and income to ensure the partnership makes the greatest profit with the fewest number of tax implications.

EXPERIENCED NEGOTIATORS IN ACTION

Negotiating with anyone, and especially with your partners, is both an art and a science. For this reason, researchers all over the world have difficulty when they study negotiators in action. However, certain generalizations can be drawn from their work. Studies have been conducted in which experienced negotiators have taken the challenge to negotiate

with much less experienced negotiators. The findings consistently show
that experienced negotiators obtain more because of the following:

- They begin with higher aspirations than inexperienced negotiators.
- They make fewer concessions throughout the negotiation process.
- They consistently make low offers, giving them more room to
  move up in their price.
- They make fewer proposals than the inexperienced negotiators.
- They have greater accuracy in judging their opponent's interests.

Let's look at each of these points closely.

High Aspirations

Experienced negotiators set a high, reasonable goal for themselves before starting their negotiations. The key word here is *reasonable*. They have
high aspirations, but not *outrageously* high aspirations and expectations.

Few Concessions

During the negotiation, experienced negotiators are more judicious
about making certain concessions than beginning negotiators. In fact,
they are not quick to concede anything. They usually offer a concession

or two only when they know they can gain specific concessions from the other side.

Consistent Offers

If a trained negotiator believes a compromise can be reached, he or she will keep the momentum of the negotiation going and give away few points, while still recognizing which factors are the most critical ones to keep. Experienced negotiators consistently craft low offers to reinforce their initial position.

Limit Number of Proposals Submitted

Experienced negotiators submit a fresh proposal or counterproposal only when they see that the negotiation has materially changed. They do not submit new proposals when only a few details have changed.

Accuracy of Judgment

Experienced negotiators tend to have greater accuracy when making judgments about the other party's interests in the deal. Because of their experience, they are much better at determining which points are the most salient to the other side. Inexperienced negotiators deal with a lot more trial and error before coming to an agreement.

SUMMARY POINTS FOR CHAPTER 5:
PARTNERS—THE OTHER HALF OF YOU

- Continually ask open-ended questions during the research phase as well as during the actual negotiation.
- When negotiating with someone who might become your partner, consider the initial investment required, the common goal of the investment, the budgets you need to set, additional capital, distribution of responsibilities, exit strategy, tax structure, and ownership structure.

- Experienced negotiators obtain more than inexperienced negotiators because they begin with higher aspirations, make fewer concessions, consistently make low offers, and allow for fewer proposals. They also have greater accuracy in judging their opponent's interests.

Come to the Table!

Asking for an Explanation

Of course, one's judgment becomes stronger over time through real-life experience. In the beginning, though, you can enhance your negotiating ability by continually asking open-ended questions during the research phase as well as during the actual negotiation. I suggest you write down a few open-ended questions and ask them at the appropriate time. Examples of questions to ask include:

- "What will happen if you can't close within 60 days?"
- "Why are you hesitant to accept my deal with only 15 percent down?"
- "What is the reason you can only accept three payments instead of four?"

Some people don't feel comfortable asking a lot of questions, but to successfully negotiate, probing for explanations is extremely important. Each time your opponent requests a concession or an adjustment to the transaction, be sure to ask the question "Why?" and follow that with several more questions. Get comfortable asking for lots of details, including the following:

- "Why do you need to close in 30 days?"
- "Why do you need six months of free rent?"
- "Can you show me how you arrived at a particular number?"

Your goal in asking all these questions is to thoroughly understand the situation and the other person's motives.

6

BANKERS—KEEPERS
OF THE COIN

During a negotiation, it would be wise not to take anything personally.
If you leave personalities out of it, you will be able to see opportunities more objectively.

Brian Koslow

The second person you will contend with is the financial professional who will supply the capital to purchase the real estate property. That person comes from the ranks of traditional bankers, mortgage bankers, mortgage brokers, and private equity fund holders, to name a few.

Obtaining the best mortgage, which includes obtaining the best interest rate and the optimal payment terms, begins with preparation. Here's one way to prepare. Although it may sound contradictory, I recommend you go to the bank where you do *not* want to obtain a loan. Applying for a loan there gives you a dress rehearsal and allows you to act more cavalier and even make mistakes. This dress rehearsal becomes a learning experience that will build your confidence and help you be better prepared when you sit down with a loan officer of the institution you choose to do business with.

Yes, this rehearsal may cost you a few dollars because you have to pay an application fee that ranges from $100 to $300. But that small investment will be worth a great deal of money to you if it helps you to negotiate well and to obtain the best mortgage deal you possibly can.

TACTICS TO USE WHEN NEGOTIATING WITH THE MONEY SOURCE

Negotiating with a banker is completely different than negotiating with a partner, a seller, or a tenant. You are actually negotiating with an institution that has many policies and procedures. Few loan officers are paid by commission or by the number of loans processed. They receive a salary so, no matter how great the interest rates and how many customers receive mortgages, loan officers get paid the same amount of money. Therefore, they have no intrinsic incentive to close a deal or work hard. I suggest you quiz loan officers about the products available and make the process easier for everyone. (To do this, you can use a matrix approach, which is described in this chapter's *Come to the Table* section.)

Given that, I suggest that the best tactics to use with bankers or loan officers are as follows:

- Research information about present interest rates and study forecasts from experts about future interest rates.
- Prepare a comprehensive financial statement (an accountant can help you with this) and bring it with you for your meeting at the bank.
- Determine what market share the bank has regarding the type of loan you are seeking. This could take time because the information is not readily available. To start, log on to the Internet and use Google or another search service. Type in the phrase "market share" and the particular bank's name to see what information it gives to the public. From that, you can develop specific questions and ask the bankers you are interviewing to answer them.
- Use the banker matrix to track your research among all the bankers you interview. (Refer to the *Come to the Table* section in this chapter.)
- Prepare the income approach analysis, which you'll find in Chapter 9 under the heading Property Valuation.

DO YOUR RESEARCH AND BE PREPARED

The motto of the U.S. Coast Guard is "Semper Paratus," which means "Always Prepared." Like the Coast Guard, to obtain the best mortgage possible, you need to get prepared. Your goal? To challenge the banker you want to work with to provide you with the best loan the bank can offer.

But before visiting the bank, I recommend that you review and print out information on available loans from HSH Financial Publishers (go to http://www.hsh.com). HSH Financial Publishers, the nation's largest publisher of consumer loans, acts as a watchdog of mortgages throughout the United States.

Tuck your research information on available mortgages into a folder and bring it with you to the appointment with the loan officer. However, I suggest that you access this information only if necessary. If the loan officer quotes rates, fees, and terms that are acceptable or better than the data you've uncovered, there's no need to discuss that data. If the loan officer doesn't give you that information, though, don't hesitate to pull it from your file.

Paying Fees

Another group of important items to research before negotiating with the bank loan officer, mortgage broker, or any other financing entity are the fees you'll have to pay. Many lending institutions and mortgage brokers charge unnecessary fees, sometimes referred to as "junk" fees. Each category of fees they charge can add up to a substantial amount of money.

An example of a "junk" fee is charging for an electronic credit check. This electronic credit check probably costs the company about $10, but the lender turns around and charges the customer much more, perhaps more than $60. When negotiating with the banker or mortgage broker, take a position to have every fee eliminated unless it can fully be substantiated by the banker or the mortgage broker. If you can't get the fee eliminated, at least try to get it reduced. Your goal should be to have each fee reduced by at least 25 percent.

Prepayment and Early Payoffs

Another important component to negotiate is the prepayment penalty or early payoff penalty. Many financial institutions impose a penalty if you pay off your loan before its due date. Your intent is to negotiate this penalty out of the deal before it's ever stated in the mortgage documents. Be clear with the bank loan officer and/or the mortgage broker on this requirement. Sometimes bankers trick you into accepting the penalty as you sign the documents. For example, you might ask to have a prepayment penalty eliminated, which the bank officer or mortgage broker obliges, but you are not told that there is an early payoff penalty, which you didn't know to ask about. Therefore, when negotiating this component of the mortgage, be explicit with your questions. Ask for information about both prepayment and early payoff penalties.

Preapproval Letters

After completing negotiations with lenders, be sure to request that they provide a preapproval letter. The letter shows prospective sellers you have been preapproved to receive a loan in order to purchase a property. The letter also should indicate how much of a mortgage they will provide you. By having this letter in hand, your negotiations with sellers will go more smoothly.

*C*ome to the *T*able!

Use a Matrix to Assess Your Best Loan Option

Using a matrix approach will aid you in your negotiations to obtain an acceptable mortgage. The matrix below cites all the elements that you will negotiate with a banker or mortgage broker. I strongly recommend that you bring the actual matrix with you and have each banker you interview fill in the blanks *using his or her own handwriting*. In my experience, doing so enhances the sense of commitment each of them feels when vying for your business.

After Banker A provides you with all of his information, go to the nearest competitor, show that person the matrix, and ask if the bank can beat the loan package that Banker A provided.

After you have Banker A and Banker B's input, go to a third bank and show the banker there the same table with the other two bankers' handwritten notes. Then ask Banker C if he or she can provide the best loan package for you.

	BANK A	BANK B	BANK C
Down payment			
Mortgage amount			
Interest rate			
Application fee			
Points			
Prepayment penalty/early payoff penalty			
Loan approval by (name of banker)			

This matrix helps you compare the policies and fees for Banks A, B, and C.

Next, leave copies of the completed matrix with the two bankers who had the least favorable loan packages and say, "I'm going to leave a copy with you; you might want to show your boss. And if you have a product that's better than this, or think you will have one coming out soon, let me know." (Note: This whole process assumes you have good creditworthiness, and that you can actually qualify for the mortgage amount.)

It's critical to note that any of these bankers can only give you the best deal within their respective bank's guidelines. However, those guidelines may be broken or altered if you provide the bank with information and proof that the bank is losing market share. Pulling together the background information for making this point may take time but you can use it as a key factor in negotiating successfully.

BANKS CAN CHANGE THEIR POSITION

In the process of negotiating deals with real estate investors, it may seem that banks take the most rigid stance about their rules compared to other sources, such as private individuals, family members, or even the sellers (who may be willing to provide financing directly as part of the sale). The following story illustrates how a bank can change its position from being rigid to being more flexible.

Bernie, the attorney who had been my legal counsel for many years, was conducting a bank closing on the purchase of a three-family house. We had all agreed to the price and terms of the sale, and I had obtained approval for the mortgage. We already had set the closing date.

At the closing—just before the important component of the paperwork was to be signed—Bernie, without giving me notice, cited statistics showing that recent mortgage rates declined. Then he stated to all parties in the room that we would not be able to close on the deal. Hearing his declaration, I was in a state of shock because I really wanted to purchase this house. Bernie continued with his explanation and stated that the interest rates had gone down, and that I was having second thoughts. He made an argument that it would be "most fair" if the bank would reduce the interest rate on the loan by a half-point.

The people sitting around the table just couldn't believe Bernie's statement. The banker responded by saying that all the paperwork was complete and the bank wasn't about to change its position. Again, diplomatically but firmly, Bernie stated that we would not continue the closing and suggested that the bank make a call to headquarters, explain the situation, and try to obtain agreement to reduce the interest rate amount. The banker left the table and made the call. When he came back, he said that he was given the authority to reduce the loan interest rate by ⅛ percentage point. Bernie and I accepted the reduction, the paperwork was changed, and we closed the deal.

In this negotiating situation, Bernie used three key qualities of experienced negotiators:

1. He had a strong conviction regarding what he believed to be fair.
2. He made statements that were indisputable.
3. He capitalized on the timing of the situation.

Truthfully, the banker personally didn't care whether I received an ⅛ percentage point reduction. And the seller and all of his representatives just wanted the deal to close. In fact, they had actually alienated other potential buyers by aligning with my attorney so that the deal would close immediately.

Now, I do not advise using this tactic at every closing. But in this case, Bernie felt strongly that the interest rates had dropped substantially and that his client (me) sat at the closing table without the benefit of the recent drop in interest rates. What's more, over the years, I had purchased many properties with Bernie and knew that he only executed this strategy this one time. I agreed that it was the appropriate tactic in this case and not a "trick." Bernie had requested a reasonable reduction and took advantage of the timing of the situation on my behalf.

NOW WHO'S THE STRONG ONE AT THE TABLE?

In negotiation, especially with bankers, a phenomenon sometimes occurs that I refer to as the "assumption of strength." People who have not been trained to be bankers and have not had finance education often feel intimidated in the company of bankers or similar professionals. They assume that the person sitting on the other side of the table negotiates from a position of strength because the loan officer may be more familiar with the disciplines of banking than he or she is.

Ironically, the opposite is often the reality. Many bankers don't call their competitors for information every day. They don't run competitive analyses on interest rates or shop around for mortgages every day, either. Yes, they are highly knowledgeable about their own bank's position and processes. But you, the educated investor who has developed a negotiating plan, have conducted in-depth research and shopped around for mortgages. Therefore, you would probably be in an even greater position of strength than the bank's representative. Never underestimate yourself and your ability to negotiate successfully.

NEGOTIATING WITH VARIOUS FINANCIAL PROFESSIONALS

In addition to negotiating with bankers, you'll likely be in negotiations with other financial professionals. Here are some points to keep in mind when dealing with various professionals, including mortgage bankers, mortgage brokers, and private equity fund owners.

Mortgage Bankers

Mortgage bankers represent companies that are willing to lend money to buy real estate properties. The important thing to keep in mind when negotiating with mortgage bankers is that they are less lenient with their requirements than banks. However, the interest rates, penalties, payments, and other fees they charge are usually much higher than what regular banks charge.

Mortgage Brokers

Mortgage brokers are a different breed than bankers and mortgage bankers. In fact, they're not bankers at all. They are the intermediaries between you and the potential sources of funding for your mortgage. Therefore, working with them is more similar to working with real estate brokers than with bankers because they're paid on commission.

When you're negotiating with mortgage brokers, be sure to emphasize how many points are required in the deal, and how many lending institutions are being approached. Why? Because you want to make sure the broker is working hard for you.

Private Equity Fund Owners

Instead of dealing with banks or mortgage companies, real estate capital can be acquired through firms that offer private equity funds, which are similar to venture capital and buyout funds. High-risk private real estate deals are often financed through private equity funds.

SUMMARY POINTS FOR CHAPTER 6: BANKERS—KEEPERS OF THE COIN

- Employ the best tactics you can with bankers or loan officers. Do your research on rates and forecasts, prepare a financial statement, determine what market share the bank has for your type of loan, use the banker matrix to track your research, and prepare the income approach analysis.

- Beware of bearing an "assumption of strength," which means assuming the banker on the other side of the table has more strength than you do. It's often not true. Never underestimate yourself and your ability to negotiate successfully.
- Keep in mind their various roles and strengths when dealing with finance professionals, including bankers, mortgage bankers, mortgage brokers, and private equity fund owners.

7

BROKERS—FINDING THE RIGHT ONES FOR YOU

Let every eye negotiate for itself and trust no agent.

William Shakespeare

The next professional that you'll be required to work with in the real estate transaction is the real estate broker. In most places, including New York City, which is my backyard, one real estate broker represents the buyer of a property and another real estate broker represents the seller. The first broker you'll negotiate with is the one who will represent *you*. Your first negotiation will be to write the contract that retains him or her to represent your interests.

The second real estate broker you will negotiate with is the one who represents the other party in the transaction. In the case of a lease transaction, the landlord will work with a representative—either a real estate broker who gets paid on commission or a licensed real estate broker who is paid a salary by the landlord. The tenants also could have real estate brokers representing them.

If you are a buyer, you may choose to negotiate the deal without a real estate broker, but I believe it is imprudent to do so. If you have not negotiated and closed numerous real estate deals, I recommend using an experienced real estate professional to assist you so you'll come out in a strong position. If the chemistry is right, you and your real estate broker can become a formidable negotiating team.

THE BROKER AND YOU—A WINNING COMBINATION

The predominant reasons to use a real estate broker when buying property include the following:

- The broker is knowledgeable about the present market.
- The broker has access to various real estate databases.
- The broker knows about the important details and subtleties of real estate transactions.
- The experienced broker has witnessed and participated in a wide variety of solutions applied to many different real estate situations over the years.
- In most real estate transactions, the seller or the landlord pays the commission, not you, the buyer.

However, if you choose to go it alone and negotiate against a real estate broker who represents the seller without a broker on your side, I suggest you get prepared in the following ways:

- Know the market
- Rein in your competition
- Strengthen your proposal
- Meet the seller

Let's examine each of these in more detail.

Know the Market

It is important to obtain as much knowledge as possible about the real estate market in the locale where you want to buy. As mentioned, a real estate broker will have access to various real estate databases and holds detailed information on all the real estate transactions that have occurred in specific locales. Some of these databases are not available to the general public. In fact, some cost their subscribers thousands of dollars a month and require users to subscribe for a minimum of a year.

Rein In Your Competition

True real estate professionals look out for their clients' best interests. Be mindful that the seller's real estate broker will solicit many potential buyers and attempt to get one to bid against the others. Simply stated, a real estate professional is trained to set up a horse race between the buyers. As a potential buyer, you're in the race!

The worst situation takes place when a real estate broker reviews your offer and shops it around. If orchestrated properly, that can run up the bidding price significantly. How can you do your best to eliminate that possibility? Before you submit your written offer on the property you want to buy, get the broker to state the price that will be accepted and ask for a commitment to that price. For example, you would start the conversation by saying, "I'm seriously thinking about providing you with an offer. What will it take to lock in the deal with both you and the seller?"

Then, after you determine the price that's acceptable to the seller and is in your budget, your written offer should begin with language like this:

"As per our discussion on _____(date), you stated that the seller would accept $_____(offer amount). This letter is to formally accept the price of $ _____ (may or may not be the same as the offer amount) to purchase the property."

The remainder of the letter should cite additional terms and conditions. This is how you rein in your competition and keep the price within your range.

Strengthen Your Proposal

Real estate brokers are constantly trying to distinguish a "prospect" (a serious buyer) from a "suspect" (someone who isn't seriously interested). One especially frustrating element a real estate broker contends with is not knowing if the buyer actually has the financial resources to purchase the property. Not surprisingly, real estate brokers will always pay the most attention to only those who can demonstrate the strength of their finances. Therefore, if you want to be taken seriously by real estate brokers, include a financial statement when you submit your offer.

Present it in the form of a preapproval letter or bank letter touting your strong financial position.

Meet the Seller

Real estate brokers often feel protective of their clients and may be reluctant to introduce you to the seller of the property. Frequently, the buyer never lays eyes on the seller until the day of the closing.

However, it may be in your best interest to meet the seller early on so you can have a face-to-face discussion. If the seller's real estate broker hesitates to set up this type of meeting, simply state that you will sign a letter recognizing that you will work through him or her to purchase the property. This should give the broker confidence that you're not trying to shortcut the process and go around him or her.

CONSIDER WHAT MOTIVATES REAL ESTATE BROKERS

If you're the buyer, I highly recommend working with an expert real estate professional to help you in your negotiations. You'll find it's just like working with your lawyer; at first your real estate broker is an *opponent* who soon becomes a *proponent*. But unlike your lawyer or banker or general contractor, your real estate broker has a different motivation: making a commission on the deal. That's important because it means your broker will only get paid if

- a transaction is completed, and
- you're satisfied and agree to the deal.

Remember, real estate brokers never want a deal to drag on. They're interested in quickly closing as many deals as possible, because the more deals that close, the more money they make. Understanding their motivation is essential to negotiating an excellent agreement.

KEY NEGOTIATION POINTS

Real estate brokers have a few printed agreements that they use; some use a short form and some have forms that can be several pages long. (See Appendix B for two versions of typical real estate brokerage agreements.) These documents are boilerplate agreements created for the broker's benefit, but they can be modified. A smart broker will work closely with you to negotiate in the terms you want and need.

> **Learn to Change Documents without Hesitation**
>
> Many investors have become accustomed to looking at a formal contract or an application that looks official and proficient, and they would never dare to mark up the text of this contract. But in business negotiations, you must become comfortable with marking up a document in pen, crossing out anything you don't agree with, adding your own recommendations, and handing it back to the other party. Be sure to initial corrections that you make on those formal-looking documents.

When negotiating with a real estate broker, keep in mind these key points:

- Setting the amount of the commission
- Determining who pays the commission
- Setting the duration of the agreement
- Having an escape clause to get out of the agreement
- Spelling out the broker's responsibilities to the buyer

Let's examine each of these in more detail.

Amount of Commission

Each real estate company publishes its commission fees in the Standard Commission Schedule. This schedule lists exactly *how* brokers get paid and sometimes *when* they get paid. I suggest you request a copy of the broker's commission schedule. If you've invested in a strong seller's market and your property is highly desirable because of its excellent condition and location, then it would be wise to negotiate for a modest reduction in the real estate broker's fee. Of course, the actual commission fee is negotiable. But be aware that reducing the fee too much may not be in your best interest.

A Word of Caution. Remember, a real estate transaction involving the sale of property usually has a commission paid by the seller. For example, let's say it's customary that a 6 percent commission fee is paid. Of that 6 percent, 3 percent goes to the buying broker and 3 percent to the selling broker. If you reduce that percentage to 5 or 4 percent, then the broker who represents you will have to tell outside brokers (who represent numerous buyers) that the commission on this particular deal is less than for most deals. If the commission is reduced to 5 percent, the broker is most likely hard-pressed to give the outside broker 3 percent and only keep 2 percent for himself. Therein lies the dilemma. So in your negotiating tactics, you can attempt to reduce the 6 percent commission fee, but be sure to agree that the outside broker will be paid the customary amount. That way, you'll get more interest from outside brokers.

Also, if you know a potential buyer and you've had discussions regarding the possibility of that person buying your property, you should bring this to the attention of the broker during the negotiating session. Be sure to list that person's name in an addendum to the agreement between you and the real estate broker. If indeed the property is sold to that person (or anyone else cited on this list), then the broker would not be eligible to earn a commission, or perhaps the broker can be given a reduced fee.

Dual Agency. A real estate broker also could be amenable to negotiating a reduced fee if the real estate broker's company acts in a dual agent capacity. A dual agent is someone who represents both you and the buyer of a particular property. In this situation, the total commission, which is normally split between your broker and an outside broker, would go solely to your broker.

What if you, the seller, find a buyer for your property yourself? Or what if you are the property owner and locate the tenants yourself? Under these circumstances, you can negotiate a slightly lower commission. However, please keep in mind that a good real estate broker will spend a substantial amount of money and time producing and placing advertisements, mailing flyers and postcards, conducting open houses, and so on. If a buyer comes to you directly, it would be unfair to attempt to negotiate a "no commission" arrangement. The truth is that you may not know exactly how the buyer knew to contact you directly. Perhaps the information came from an ad or a flyer that your broker circulated, but the buyer took the initiative to call you directly instead of calling the broker.

Who Pays the Commission?

The payment of real estate brokerage commissions varies; there is no one standard in the United States for their payment. However, several factors come into play to determine who pays.

Customarily, in a typical real estate transaction of a home or small property, the seller pays the commission. That amount gets split between the broker who represents the seller and the broker who represents the buyer. In a leasing transaction, landlords usually pay their in-house broker as well as the broker who brings in the tenants.

In extremely large real estate transactions—for example, the sale of a skyscraper in a major city—paying the commission may be the responsibility of both the buyer and the seller. In fact, it is common for the seller's broker to obtain a commission from the seller and the buyer's broker to obtain a commission from the buyer.

Before negotiating the rate of commission, do your homework on what is customary and standard in the area where the property is located. To find out what is standard, call at least five real estate brokerage companies and ask for an overview of how commissions are commonly paid, both for a property purchase and a lease transaction. Arm yourself with good information you can use in your negotiations.

Duration of Agreement

Generally, brokers want exclusive agreements with their clients for six months to one year. I suggest you follow a logical approach, explaining that you need the assignment (i.e., the property to be sold, bought, or leased) accomplished in 60 days (or whatever time frame is required). Logically, the term of the agreement should be the length of time needed to complete the assignment itself. This then becomes an "indisputable."

In some situations or locales, transactions often take longer than anticipated, so it's best to cut the broker some slack by adding in an extra month beyond the target accomplishment date to the contract date.

Escape Clause to Get out of the Agreement

Another way to declare an "indisputable" is to obtain an escape or exit clause. Simply say to the broker, "I believe that if the business relationship between us is not working, it will not make sense to continue it. How do we address this issue?" A professional broker with integrity would respond by saying he or she should not be working for you if you're not satisfied with the service and performance you're receiving.

What should your intent be? Would you feel most comfortable if you could terminate the agreement without cause? If so, also state that you'll give the broker a 30-day notice to officially terminate the agreement. This arrangement gives the real estate broker a fair amount of time to correct or cure any shortcomings.

Broker's Responsibilities to the Buyer

Your contract with the broker should explain what he or she will do to assist you in the transaction. It should cover such items as the following:

- Accessing the Multiple Listings Services (MLS) and other real estate databases
- Advertising the property in specific publications
- Keeping a written record of prospects
- Creating fliers or brochures
- Conducting direct mail and telephone campaigns
- Conducting open houses
- Creating a Web site
- Sending out news releases

TO SIGN OR NOT TO SIGN

Some buyers and sellers prefer not to sign an agreement with a real estate broker. Instead, they attempt to negotiate an oral agreement.

Worse than that, they insist brokers run around town looking for space for them without signing an agreement.

On the surface, this may seem like a good strategy for those interested in buying property; instead of making a commitment to one broker, these buyers have many brokers looking for them. But this is the worst strategy that a buyer can employ. Here's why.

To recognize the pitfalls of this strategy, you must understand the nuances of the real estate brokerage industry. All real estate brokers have two stacks of paper on their desks. One pile contains agreements from all the customers who have made a commitment to them and to whom they've made a commitment in return. Experience has shown that if these brokers can successfully satisfy the real estate needs of any customer represented in that pile, they will be paid a commission. Remember, brokers are not on salary—their income is driven by commissions.

The second pile represents information about people who have not made a commitment to any real estate broker. Brokers know that these people are running around town with more than one broker to help them. If a sweet deal or a good opportunity comes into the real estate brokerage company, which pile do you think a broker turns to first? Which would you turn to if you were in a broker's position?

Do You Want to Get Good Service?

I'm amused when prospective clients declare that there are no good deals in town, exclaiming, "Everything the brokers show me is terrible. There are no good deals out there at all!" I always ask my prospective clients if they've hired a real estate broker to assist them. Usually their answer is, "I don't want to hire anyone in particular. I want to broaden my horizons and keep my options open." Of course, brokers know this type of client won't be committed to buying from them, so they show the buyer below-standard opportunities and spend a minimum amount of time with them.

The bottom line? If you want real estate brokers to be committed to you and your needs, get committed to them by signing agreements with them.

The Unsettling Indisputable Declaration

At times during a negotiation, you might see an opening just ready for you to walk through it. To the quarterbacks of a football team, it's the clearing of the field and the unencumbered view to throw the football downfield. To boxers, it's the millisecond their opponent lets down his guard. And in negotiations, you'll learn to see similar opportunities and to take advantage of favorable moments.

If you are the buyer (or representing the buyer) and you're dealing in a buyer's market, look for a way to make an "unsettling indisputable declaration" that will ring clearly and loudly in the negotiation room. If it's indisputably a buyer's market—touted as such in the newspapers and television—capitalize on that fact! That can mean the first thing you might say when you enter the negotiation room filled with all of the parties is, "Good morning everyone. Thank you for joining us. Because it's a buyer's market, we're anxious to get started today."

Try that tactic. You'll see that this simple statement becomes an unsettling declaration. And it's a brave person who tries to dispute a statement that's wrapped in such pleasantry. Most people won't challenge you if everyone in the room recognizes that the market has been and will be in the buyer's favor. The benefit? It demonstrates your confidence and your knowledge that you're negotiating from a position of strength.

SUMMARY POINTS FOR CHAPTER 7: BROKERS—FINDING THE RIGHT ONES FOR YOU

- It's wise to use the services of real estate brokers when buying properties because they're knowledgeable about the markets, they have access to various real estate databases, they know about the important details and subtleties of real estate transactions, and they have participated in and witnessed a wide variety of solutions applied to many different real estate situations over the years. In addition, in most transactions, the seller or the landlord pays the commission, not you, the buyer.
- If you choose to work without the services of a broker, at a minimum be sure you study the market, rein in your competition, strengthen your proposal, and meet the seller in the early stages.

- Tap into a real estate broker's motivation to close the deal quickly for the highest amount possible: earning a good commission fast.
- Get comfortable marking up a document in pen, crossing out anything you don't agree with, adding your own recommendations, and handing it back to the other party.
- When negotiating with a real estate broker, consider the amount of the commission, who pays it, the duration of the agreement, having an escape clause to get out of the agreement, and spelling out the broker's responsibilities to the buyer.
- I strongly recommend you sign an agreement to create an exclusive relationship with the real estate broker you want to hire.

8

LAWYERS—CAGING THE LEGAL EAGLES

I had never even thought I'd be an actress–I was supposed to be a lawyer.
But the motivation is the same: when you act, you defend a role; you have to be convincing.
It's the same career.

Anne Parillaud

Regarding the real estate transaction process, lawyers are important and necessary professionals. Selecting the right lawyer to work with is critical, especially if you intend to buy and sell more than one property in your lifetime.

PRELIMINARY ELEMENTS WHEN INTERVIEWING ATTORNEYS

For every attorney you interview as a professional to work with, I suggest you negotiate several preliminary elements or negotiating points that include the following:

- Legal fee
- Capping the fee
- Out-of-pocket expenses
- Retainer
- Payment schedule
- Responsibilities
- Time line/schedule

Let's review each of these items.

Legal Fee

Similar to the real estate transaction itself, striving to obtain the lowest-priced legal fee may not be your best choice. Of course, you don't want to overpay for legal fees. You'll find, however, that legal fees can be highly negotiable because, unlike real estate property, no independent source compares the legal fees of different law firms. Sometimes you'll see the phrase "customary and reasonable legal fees" in a legal document. Beware: What is considered customary and reasonable ranges widely. You'll want to retain competent legal services at the lowest *cost-effective* price.

Capping the Fee

The dollar-per-hour payment arrangement means that the lawyer, and sometimes the junior lawyer, who works on your transaction will track every hour they spend on your real estate deal. Without capping this fee, you can be riding a runaway train. Often, busy lawyers can't give you an up-to-the-minute report on how much you owe for their services. In fact, it will be difficult for you to dispute how many hours the lawyers actually worked on your behalf. Therefore, the preferred payment schedule for real estate transactions is a flat fee—one number only.

If you can't get your lawyer to agree on a fixed flat fee, then it's important to get an agreement to cap the fee. For example, you would say, "Mr. Smith agrees to charge $50 per hour to provide legal services to close on this deal. However, he will cap the fee at a maximum of $1,700. I will also agree to pay a minimum of $1,200."

Negotiating this type of payment structure will give you the peace of mind that your legal fee will not run over your budget. It also gives your lawyer a degree of comfort, knowing that he or she will receive a known minimum payment.

Out-of-Pocket Expenses

Many lawyers attempt to negotiate for coverage of out-of-pocket expenses, which are items like paying for messengers, postage, copying, faxing, and so on. These expenses may seem insignificant, but they can add up. Your reply back to the lawyer should be an indisputable. For example, you could say, "The reason I'm considering hiring you as my attorney for all of my real estate transactions is because of your vast experience. It's my understanding that you've done many transactions similar to mine. Therefore, you must know from your experience how much out-of-pocket expenses could be. I request that the fixed amount we agree to include those items."

Retainer and Payment Schedule

Many professionals only start to provide services once they receive a partial payment up front. This is a fair request. I suggest you try to negotiate 25 percent of the total cost or less as a retainer.

After you agree to pay a flat fee without any out-of-pocket expenses, you then negotiate the payment schedule. You could offer the following schedule:

- 25 percent retainer
- 25 percent at the closing
- 25 percent 30 days later
- 25 percent 60 days later

Once agreed on, I strongly suggest you put the fee schedule in writing. This avoids allowing the lawyer to create a loophole in the fee payments and also tests his or her practical sense. For follow up, I recommend that you send the lawyer a letter agreeing to the fee.

Responsibilities

People often think they've hired their lawyers to do all their negotiating for them. That's dropping the ball and failing to take responsibility. Don't do it! Your lawyer should come in *after* the meat of negotiation is complete. A lawyer's job is to protect your interests. It's *your* job to do the initial legwork and hammer out the details, and then give the terms and conditions to your lawyer to refine. Your lawyer's job is to negotiate the legal nuances on your behalf.

Specifically, your lawyer should be responsible for drafting and reviewing proposals, counterproposals, brokerage agreements, side letters, and the contract of sale. He or she also provides all services related to the closing of the transaction, which includes appearing at the closing.

Schedule

In your agreement with your lawyer, include time lines for the process to take place. For example, you may want to add the following into the agreement:

"Lawyer will help to negotiate the transaction and create the term sheet by _____.

Lawyer will prepare all closing documents by _____.

Lawyer will attend closing, which should be scheduled on or before _____."

HOW TO CHOOSE A LAWYER TO WORK WITH

Negotiations fall into two categories. The first category is comprised of people you're forced to negotiate with. For example, if you work in a corporation, it's rare to be able to choose your supervisor when it comes time to negotiate a promotion or salary increase. The second category of negotiation is with people you can select, such as your lawyer. To make your negotiations with a lawyer easier, find appropriate candidates to consider, then choose a professional who will become your proponent.

I suggest you use a matrix approach, like the one below, anytime you're dealing with a professional who's not paid by commission or driven by incentives. Because real estate brokers are paid by commissions, a matrix approach doesn't work with them, but it will work with lawyers. When shopping around for a lawyer, a matrix helps you compare those you interview and easily view all the points you're negotiating. That includes dollar-per-hour versus flat fee, payment schedule, cap fee, retainer fee, out-of-pocket expenses, senior versus junior lawyer, and so on. Beyond getting a good price, this approach gives you an opportunity to see them in action and learn about their negotiating abilities.

To get started, first ask friends and colleagues for referrals. In particular, ask them how much they are paying for the legal services they're receiving. Then create and use a matrix to compare at least three lawyers who are referred to you.

	LAWYER		
	A	**B**	**C**
Legal fee: $/hour			
Legal fee: Flat fee			
Capping the fee			
Out-of-pocket expenses			
Payment schedule			
Responsibilities			
Time line/schedule			

LOOK FOR OPERATION INDICATORS

In addition to the categories you've noted in the matrix, assess how a lawyer treats you as a prospective client. That can indicate how he or she would treat other parties in your real estate negotiations. Also, be wary of a lawyer who is indecisive about fees and takes too long to return calls. This isn't a good sign! With lawyers, the characteristics of slowness, indecision, and vagueness increase the number of hours they will take to complete transactions, thereby increasing the amount of money you'd have to pay if you're invoiced on an hourly basis.

Here are some "operation indicators" that will help you choose the best lawyer.

Play the Referral Card

Keep in mind that smart lawyers know they need to constantly increase their client base, plus they want clients to keep coming back and referring more business. I suggest you make this a point of leverage in your negotiations. However, to do this, you must genuinely know people who may need their legal services. Note that I stress the word "may"; I believe it's neither necessary nor prudent to *guarantee* any client future referrals.

Be Sure to Meet in Person

I recommend you negotiate details of a new relationship as much as you can on the phone. However, before you sign off on the fee schedule, meet with each of the lawyers you may hire face to face. Contracting with a lawyer over the phone or through e-mail simply isn't wise.

Consider the Chemistry

Even though one lawyer may charge more than the others for each real estate closing, that lawyer may have the chemistry and patience that matches your personality, as well as the skills that match your needs. Paying a little more for what seems to work best goes a long way and will pay off in the long run.

Research Firms Thoroughly

Do a lot of research on each of the law firms that you are considering. I recommend using Internet search services like Google and Yahoo! to conduct background checks on each of the law firms with which you'll negotiate.

Select Seniors, Not Juniors

Sometimes a senior lawyer will speak with you and negotiate the fee agreement, but the actual work will be done by someone much more junior. In your negotiations for retaining a lawyer, especially from a big firm, specify that no junior person be assigned to you for client service. Be sure that you're receiving the service you are paying for. It's wise to ask the lawyers on your consideration list for references of clients they've successfully served. Always follow up and call those clients, making a point of asking which lawyer in the firm actually did the work.

Come to the Table!

Take a Proactive Stance

In negotiating, you can either take a proactive stance or a reactive stance against others in any situation. It's especially important to take a proactive stance in negotiations with lawyers. Here's an example of a proactive negotiating script in dealing with a lawyer:

"I was referred to you by a past client. (Note: Don't give details about the person's actual name, address, and so on.) I'm seeking professional legal advice regarding a real estate transaction.

"Do you specialize in real estate, and if so, what specific areas? What is your fee to help me in my particular situation?"

If the lawyer provides you with a dollar-per-hour amount, you can say, "I am very budget minded so I prefer a flat fee that has a cap. Do you do that?"

Wait for the lawyer's answer.

When a flat fee is stated, politely say, "That amount is much more than I expected. I was hoping to pay X." (X should be something you are genuinely willing to pay. Usually it's 10 to 20 percent less than the flat fee initially stated.)

If the lawyer insists on charging a flat fee, ask him or her to take the time to break down the number of hours it will take to finish the real estate transaction. Once you see the breakdown, ask if you can both agree on the number of hours it will take. (You may want to add a few hours as a cushion.) Then ask to cap the project at the agreed-on number of hours.

Your ideal dialogue with the lawyer would go something like:

"Can you take a moment to list each aspect of the real estate transaction you'll be involved in and the range of hours it will take to complete each phase of the transaction?"

Listen carefully and write down the reply. It may be something like:

Review of proposals:	1 to 2 hours
Review of contract of sale:	1 to 2 hours
Negotiating contract of sale:	2 to 4 hours
Review of title and other documents:	1 to 2 hours
Attendance at the closing:	2 to 4 hours
Total	**7 to 14 hours**

(Please note: This is merely an example of how the dialogue could go. Legal fees vary greatly depending on the size and complexity of the transaction and the particular state in which the transaction will occur.)

After receiving this information, your reply should be to reemphasize that your transaction is standard, that there's nothing extraordinary about it. State that you would be willing to cap the hours at nine hours, which means convincing the lawyer to invoice you for no more than nine hours to complete your real estate transaction.

CHECKLIST FOR CHOOSING A LAWYER

Here is the basic checklist for negotiating with a lawyer in the process of selecting the one you will work with:

- Ask friends and colleagues for referrals.
- Research lawyers and their firms on the Internet.
- Visit each law firm under consideration.
- Build a matrix.
- Review the situation with each lawyer.
- Discuss a flat fee.
- Discuss the dollar-per-hour fee.
- Discuss out-of-pocket expenses.
- Cap the fee.
- Define a payment schedule.
- Ask for client references.
- Draft fee agreement.

Refer to this checklist every step of the way.

SUMMARY POINTS FOR CHAPTER 8: LAWYERS—CAGING THE LEGAL EAGLES

- Negotiate preliminary elements with a lawyer that include a legal fee, capping the fee, out-of-pocket expenses, retainer, payment schedule, responsibilities, and scheduling.

- Paying attention to operation indicators will help you make the best selection. Indicators include having potential for referrals, meeting in person, enjoying good chemistry, doing background research on the firms, and working with senior partners.
- Refer to the checklist to make sure you thoroughly cover all aspects of selecting a lawyer.

9

SELLERS—MAKING THEM FEEL COMFORTABLE

Well, real estate is always good, as far as I'm concerned.
Donald Trump

The seller of a property can be one individual, a partnership, or a corporation.

The first and most critical aspect of negotiating directly with the seller is to uncover the motivation behind his or her decision to sell the property. This can be achieved through a mild form of bonding, rather than through rapid-fire interrogation.

When meeting another person, it's human nature to immediately look at the differences between you. But when negotiating with a seller, it's advisable to change this inclination and look for similarities between the two of you in a casual way. Making the seller feel comfortable is an important art that will help you in your negotiations.

ELEMENTS OF TIMING

When negotiating for real estate property or any other big-ticket item, most people focus on price. For some reason, buyers believe that's the most important consideration from the sellers' points of view. But often that's not true—price is just *one* of the many facets to negotiate.

Come to the Table!

Striking Similarities

If you are visiting the people you'll be negotiating with in their home or office, you may notice pictures of children on the bookshelves. Perhaps they're dressed in baseball uniforms or ballerina outfits. Take the time to strike up a conversation about the kids and show a genuine interest in sharing some similarities between their children and yours. I've spent a longer time in conversations with sellers talking about similar hobbies before starting the negotiations than I have in the actual negotiations. It's a natural way to build rapport.

On the other hand, don't look for big differences between you. For example, don't say, "I see you have kids. That's too much for me. I would never have kids. How can you handle a full-time job and still manage to raise children?" Or if you see the other person is a big boating enthusiast and you're not, it would be unwise to say, "Boating is dangerous. I would never do it. In fact, I can't even swim." Be diplomatic!

An especially critical element in negotiations is timing because it affects the sellers' priorities. Is their primary objective to obtain the best price or is it to sell the property within a particular time frame?

It's critical that you determine if the sellers have a deadline, especially one that's coming up fast and can't be moved. If you have an open-ended schedule or no deadline at all, your best strategy is to ask a point-blank question: "Are you under any deadline to complete this transaction?" This tactic cannot backfire. If the question is turned back to you, which it will be, your reply should be a confident "No."

In my experience, deadlines always mean duress. Duress can cause people to concede their price considerations in greater amounts and in a faster period than when they're not. This forms the essence of why it's important to determine if a critical deadline looms. Once you've been told their actual deadline, I suggest you fashion probing questions in a specific way. For example, if your opponents insist on a 30-day close, you should ask, "Is there some specific reason why we can't agree to a more reasonable period, say 90 days?" Then find out more about the situation—this can certainly affect how you proceed with your negotiation. Specifically, find out what the 30-day deadline is related to. Perhaps the sellers just lost a job or landed a new job and have to move quickly. Perhaps they're being forced to sell because of an impending divorce or a need to relocate due to health reasons. Don't make up possible reasons—find out exactly what's going on!

HAVE A BACKUP OFFER IF YOU FACE A DEADLINE

Let's put the shoe on the other foot. Say you want to give the sellers your own deadline. This can be a double-edged sword. Suppose you include the following text in your offer: "This offer is good until April 20th at 5:00 PM. After this time, the offer is null and void." Then April 20th comes and goes. What do you do? Do the sellers call your bluff? Do they have another buyer lined up? It's hard to tell.

One tactic that may keep you in the deal and save face for both parties is to say, "You must have a better offer. If I were you, I would always take a better offer. Here is a letter that will act as a backup if your other deal falls through." Then give them a letter that details the exact terms as your last offer as in the sample letter in Figure 9.1.

PROPERTY VALUATION (OR HOW'D YOU GET THAT NUMBER?)

Sellers rarely use mathematical calculations to determine the price of their property. Unless they're under duress, most sellers approach the pricing of their property in a nonscientific way. For example, they research (or hear via the grapevine) what similar properties have sold for, then add on a random sum to arrive at their asking price. Sellers naturally want the price "the other guy" received, saying, "The next door neighbor got this much; I want more." or "The broker told me it's worth this much. I want more." In some situations, it can seem as though they're picking the number they state right out of the air.

I suggest you, the buyer, use a more scientific approach than that. However, don't say, "This is the price I'm willing to pay because this is the price I'm willing to pay." or "This is the price I want because that's all the money I have. That's my budget. I'm not spending any more."

FIGURE 9.1 *Sample Backup Letter*

(Buyer's name and address)
(City, State, Zip code)
(Date)

(Sellers of the property)
c/o (The sellers' lawyer)
(Address)
(City, State, Zip code)

Re: _____(city, state) (the "Property")

Dear _____:

The undersigned hereby reiterates our strong interest in purchasing the Property.

You have advised us that you have entered into a Contract of Sale (the "Existing Contract") with an undisclosed third-party purchaser, which Existing Contract is conditioned on a due diligence inspection the results of which are satisfactory to the purchaser therein.

Notwithstanding the existence of the Existing Contract, the undersigned is ready, willing, and able to purchase the Property for $(amount) dollars all cash, ten percent (10%) down on signing, fourteen (14) days due diligence, a time of the essence closing, and on other terms mutually acceptable to you and the undersigned. Accordingly, the undersigned is hereby requesting that you issue to us a Contract that will be (a) subordinate to the Existing Contract and (b) subject to and conditioned upon the closing pursuant to the Existing Contract not occurring, so that the rights and obligations of you and the undersigned under our Contract will terminate if and when the closing under the Existing Contract occurs.

In connection therewith, the undersigned covenants and agrees that it will not, in any way, interfere with the Existing Contract and the rights and obligations of the parties thereunder including, but not limited to, the rights of the purchaser thereunder to conduct its due diligence inspection of the Property. In furtherance thereof, the undersigned and _____ personally hereby agree to indemnify, defend, and hold you and (name real estate brokers) (and your and their partners, shareholders, members, agents, and employees) harmless from and against any loss, liability, costs, or expenses (including, but not limited to, attorneys' fees) arising from any claim or allegation that the undersigned has interfered with the rights and obligations of the parties under the Existing Contract, such agreement to indemnify, defend, and hold harmless to survive the execution and delivery of this Letter Agreement. Your partners, members, shareholders, agents, and employees, and (name the brokers) and its partners, members, shareholders, agents, and employees shall be deemed third-party beneficiaries of your agreement to indemnify, defend, and hold harmless as set forth above.

Very truly yours,

(Buyer's name)

By:_____

Accepted and agreed to:
_____

Source: © George F. Donohue

That approach simply doesn't work in negotiations. In fact, if you say it this way, you come across sounding like a stubborn child. It's more powerful to explain *how* you arrived at your position and the price you're offering. The following will give you some concrete ideas.

MATHEMATICAL CALCULATIONS

Generally speaking, if one party uses an unreasonable method of arriving at a position, it leads to an unreasonable discussion on that particular item. To contend with any element of the negotiation in which no calculations or reasons are given, learn how to use mathematical calculations. More than that, learn how to apply them to your advantage.

In buying and selling real estate, much of the negotiation factors on evaluating the property, so understanding how to arrive at the value of a property becomes paramount. Professional appraisers commonly use these three approaches to assess the value of properties:

1. The income approach
2. The market approach
3. The replacement approach

In preparing your negotiation plan against the seller, first explore each of these approaches and determine the value of the property in each of these scenarios. Next decide if you'll discuss and present one, two, or all three of these methods in your negotiation plan. Remember, real estate markets change. Prices go up and down. The income for the building can change, the market can change, and the cost of bricks and mortar can change. Therefore, don't use all of these approaches in your negotiation plan unless they can be positioned to strengthen your plan. Instead, use the best one.

Let's examine each of these approaches and see how they can be practically applied in a negotiation with the seller.

Using the Income Approach

When using the income approach—the approach I prefer—a property's value is determined by taking the amount of income the property produces (or will produce) and dividing it by a particular percentage.

This percentage reflects what the return on the building will be, which is often referred to as the capitalization rate.

Now, you won't find the particular percentage I mentioned in any newspaper or magazine, nor is it established by an authoritative institution. The percentage you use in the income approach should be similar to or greater than the percentage return that you could get from other investments, such as stocks and bonds.

For example, suppose a three-story building produces an income of $36,000 a year with expenses of $26,000 a year. The net operating income of the building is $10,000 a year.

Therefore, the calculation would look like this:

$$\frac{\text{Net operating income}}{\text{Percent}} = \text{The value of the property percent}$$

In this scenario, I chose 7 percent because I considered the return of a certificate of deposit (CD), stock, or bond to be somewhere in the range of 3 percent to 7 percent interest paid. That means if I took $142,857 and invested it in a stock that had a 7 percent dividend, I would also receive $10,000 a year:

$$\frac{\$10,000}{.07} = \$142,857$$

A second method, which determines the value of a property by its income, is more precise. Instead of using a capitalization rate or the gross rent multiplier to determine the value, I prefer to examine each of the following factors:

- All of the income the property will produce
- All of the expenses to operate the building
- The bank's perspective on what it will lend you
- The amount of money you're willing to put in as a down payment

Here is how the value is arrived at:

Gross income − Expenses = Net operating income
$36,000 − $26,000 = $10,000

$$\frac{\text{Net operating income}}{\text{Debt coverage ratio}} = \text{Annual debt amount}$$

$$\frac{\$10,000}{1.25} = \$8,000$$

$$\frac{\text{Annual debt amount}}{\text{Interest rate}} = \text{Total mortgage amount}$$

$$\frac{\$8,000}{.07} = \$114,285$$

Total mortgage amount + How much you have to put
down = Maximum price you will pay
$114,285 + $50,000 = $164,285

Using the Market Approach

Of the three approaches, the market approach is the method most people are familiar with. It uses comparables, which are the prices of one or more similar buildings that were sold recently. In a capitalistic society like we have in the United States, supply and demand usually dictate market price. But sometimes markets become irrational, or what Federal Reserve Chairman Alan Greenspan describes as "irrational exuberance." That's why this approach isn't always the best one to use.

Here's an example of using the market approach to arrive at the value of property:

1. Property A was sold three months ago for $150,000.
2. Property B was sold six months ago for $160,000.
3. Property C was sold four months ago for $155,000.

Taking the average price of the three properties, which are properties most similar to the one in question, the value of the property would be $155,000.

Using the Replacement Approach

The third approach used to evaluate a property is the replacement approach. This simply means pricing it according to what it would cost if you were to purchase the land, design the building, and construct the building exactly the way the property in question was constructed.

To use the replacement approach, have a general contractor or builder provide you with an estimate of how much the building would cost if it were built on a vacant lot next door to the property in question. For example, let's say that the three-story property has 1,500 square feet on each floor, for a total of 4,500 square feet. If the going rate to design and build a new building, including the land, is $40 per square foot, then the replacement value of the building would be as follows:

$$4,500 \text{ square feet} \times \$40 \text{ per square foot} = \$180,000$$

Comparing the Three Methods

Suppose you've examined the three methods of determining the value of a property. Using the income approach, you arrived at a value of $142,857 to $164,285; using the market approach, you arrived at a value of $155,000; and using the replacement approach, you arrived at a value of $180,000—all for the same property. You can see how easily the range of values can vary depending on the property's income, the market conditions, and the cost of new construction.

Calculating each of these values provides you with the range of numbers that your negotiations will most likely involve. Remember that those you will negotiate against may be astute, sophisticated real estate investors who also use these approaches to determine their range of negotiation—and do so more frequently than you do.

Depending on your particular circumstance and the geographic market that you're in, you may prefer to stick with one, two, or all three of these approaches when you're engaged in the negotiation.

Come to the Table!

Determining an Offer Price

Most people will characterize property simply by its price—by only one number. You may be able to gain an edge if you characterize your offer in a different manner. For example, say you're negotiating to buy a three-story building that has 2,000 square feet on each floor and has an asking price of $360,000. You could characterize the asking price in three different ways:

1. Price per building = $360,000 for the building
2. Price per floor = $120,000 per floor
3. Price per square foot = $60 per square foot

Let's compare this building with two other buildings for sale at higher asking prices.

| | Property | | |
	A	B	C
Asking price	$360,000	$375,000	$385,000
Number of floors	3	3	3
Total square feet	6,000	6,700	6,900
Dollars per floor	$120,000	$125,000	$128,333
Dollar per square foot	$60	$56	$56

This matrix helps you compare the three properties before purchasing one. After looking carefully at the elements of each property in the comparison table, you can determine how best to characterize the pricing.

In this example, the seller is trying to sell Property A for $360,000. The seller's position is that many similar buildings, such as Property B and Property C, are being sold for more than $360,000. Therefore, the seller insists that the buyer (you) come up on your offer price.

I suggest you focus your counteroffer on the dollars per square foot. In fact, hammer this point home by engaging in a dialogue that goes something like this: "Mike, you need to look closer at the details of the buildings you're drawing comparisons to. The two properties you mentioned yesterday are good suggestions. However, I did some research on these properties. If you do the calculations, you will find both buildings have an asking price of $56 per square foot. Let me stress these are the *asking* prices. If I purchased your building for the same price—that is, at $56 per square foot—the total would come to $336,000 (6,000 square feet × $56/square foot = $336,000). Because these are asking prices, the true price should be approximately 10 percent less than that. Therefore, I'm prepared to purchase your building for $303,000."

The purpose of this tactic is not to say, "Always negotiate in terms of dollars per square foot." Rather, it's to encourage you to examine all the ways a price can be characterized and then choose the one that is most advantageous to you. In some cases, it might be sticking to the asking price of the property; in other cases, it could be the dollar-per-floor price or the dollar-per-room price.

A PRICE-REDUCING TOOL

When negotiating with sellers to purchase their property, have a few negotiating tools at the ready. I consider one of the best tools to be the inspector's report. You'll need to spend a few hundred dollars to have the property you're interested in inspected by an experienced building inspector. If the building is larger than a three-family house, you may want to hire a professional inspector who's also a licensed engineer.

The cost of inspections varies, but it proves to be inexpensive compared to the value you'll receive from the report. Please note that building inspectors are not required to assess the cost estimate for necessary repairs. Rather, their job is to supply you with the report of the condition of the building on that particular day. The report should list all of the good attributes as well as the defects and code violations, if any. However, in a polite way, you can ask the inspector for a favor and request a rough estimate for repairing particular items. Have the inspector write down those items on a separate page.

This list becomes golden in your negotiations. Realize that experienced building inspectors look at every square inch of the building. If general contractors performed the same inspection, they'd likely give you estimates that are padded because it is in their best interest to obtain the highest possible price for their services. More likely than not, the general contractor's estimate will not be as detailed as a building inspector's.

Bring the building inspector's list of cost estimates with you to the negotiations and use it as a price-reducing tool. For example, you might say during the negotiation, "Mr. Jones, I hired a local licensed building inspector to carefully examine each component of your property. I have a list of necessary repairs and the cost estimate to make each repair. The total cost is $15,000, therefore, the first thing I need to do is to take at least $15,000 off the asking price."

Negotiating in the Ring

Due to the successes in my real estate career, I've traveled to 40 countries, lived abroad, driven a race car, navigated my boat through all kinds of weather, owned two restaurants, studied calligraphy and martial arts, published a book on poetry, and also took up the hobby of boxing as a young man.

During my boxing days, a friend of the family who was a golden gloves boxer offered to train me in the art of fisticuffs. That's how I realized that boxing has some inherent similarities to negotiating.

When boxing an opponent, I would break down the match into three components. The first component would be to determine the opponent's range of defenses by making short jabs to various parts of his body. Doing this determined the strength of my opponent's defense, so I could see how far he could swing his arms up or down, left or right.

The second component of the match involves locating the weaknesses of my opponent. For a right-handed opponent, I'd strike the left shoulder continually until I'd weaken that point and, therefore, weaken his defenses. The third and final component was to decide the timing for my final blow.

Negotiating and boxing are both about continually determining your opponent's range of defenses, continually weakening that defense, and then—and at the appropriate time—striking the last blow.

Let's transfer this lesson to your negotiation with a seller. You need to determine where the seller's weaknesses are (for example, during the walk-through of the building, point out each defect in the building and be sure the seller acknowledges them), then look the seller in the eye and review your list of defects out loud—deliver the final blow.

ASK THY NEIGHBOR—ACCESS TO SELLERS' MOTIVATION

Every block in every town around the world has a "block mayor," someone who is usually a self-appointed overseer, often an individual who has lived on the block the longest. I recommend that you seek out this person as well as some neighbors who live on the same block as the building you want to purchase. Strike up conversations with them and try to determine the following:

- How long has the building been on the market?
- What are the tenants in the building like?
- What is going on in the neighborhood?
- Why is the building owner selling?

The information you obtain from the neighbors will be extremely valuable, especially if it provides you further insight into the motivation of the sellers.

SUBMITTING OFFERS AND CONTRACT OF SALE

Once you've completed your research and determined a price, it's time to submit an offer to purchase the property. (See Appendix C for the form I use to submit offers.)

The contract of sale is drawn up by one of the lawyers once the buyer and seller have agreed to the material terms and conditions of the real estate transaction. The elements that will be negotiated in the contract of sale include the following:

- Amount of the earnest money
- Who will hold the earnest money
- Rate of interest on the earnest money
- Terms in which earnest money may be refunded or forfeited
- Contingency clauses
- How the balance of the purchase will be paid
- What happens if the property is not delivered to the closing
- Losses related to the good title

- Limitations on the title
- How the seller or buyer will pay or receive credits, taxes, etc.

Who **P**ays the **F**ees at **C**losing?

Traditionally, paying the closing fees falls on the buyer. If you find that the seller is highly motivated to sell, and the actual sale of the property will result in a windfall, you may want to negotiate that the seller pays all the fees.

For example, you may state to the seller or the seller's broker the following: "I recognize that you want to close within a short period of time. I am aware that you purchased your home for $80,000 ten years ago and we've agreed that I'll purchase it for $200,000. I can go forward with the closing if you are willing to pick up all the fees related to this transaction. With such a big profit, consider that it may be more prudent for you to pick up the fees for income tax purposes."

CREATING A PURCHASE AGREEMENT

Sometimes a property can be obtained along with the purchase of a business. Again, the importance of putting the material terms and conditions of a negotiation in writing is important. Figure 9.2 shows a sample agreement to purchase a business with the property. From this agreement, the lawyers will fashion a formal contract.

SUMMARY POINTS FOR CHAPTER 9:
SELLERS—MAKING THEM FEEL COMFORTABLE

- When negotiating with a seller, it's advisable to look for similarities between the two of you in a casual way.
- Always find out about the sellers' situation, especially if they've set a tight deadline. The right information can certainly affect how you proceed with your negotiation.
- If you have to set a deadline, you can protect your interests by having a backup offer. Put it in the form of a letter or proposal.

FIGURE 9.2 *Sample Business Purchase Agreement*

**Sample Business Purchase Agreement
between Dr. Alex Brown (AB) and Dr. John Day (JD)**

The following terms and conditions have been agreed to between AB and JD as a basis for the purchase of the practice presently owned and operated by JD.

1. Purchase price is $60,000.
2. Along with the execution of this agreement, AB will submit a nonrefundable good faith deposit of $6,000.
3. Purchase includes attached list and patient list.
4. Lease will be assigned to AB according to the provisions of the over lease. AB will give JD a separate check toward the security deposit that is now held in escrow by the landlord. Existing security deposit will be credited to AB.
5. Closing to be held on or before October 31, 200__.
6. JD attests that there are no outstanding litigations, debts, or any other outstanding liabilities against the practice.
7. All receivables related to the treatment of patients up until the day before the closing shall be received by JD.
8. The property will be transferred to AB for the additional sum of $100,000.

Agreed to:

_____   _____

Dr. Alex Brown   As of this date:

_____   _____

Dr. John Day   As of this date:

Source: © George F. Donohue

- Professional appraisers commonly use three approaches to value properties: the income approach, the market approach, and the replacement approach.
- Do some soft research and strike up conversations with neighbors living in the area where you want to buy a building. Ask them about how long the building has been on the market, what the tenants are like, what is going on in the neighborhood, why the building owner is selling, and so on.

- Negotiate the contract of sale and include the amount of the earnest money, who will hold the earnest money, the rate of interest on the earnest money, terms in which the earnest money may be refunded or forfeited, contingency clauses, how the balance of the purchase will be paid, what happens if the property is not delivered to the closing, losses related to the good title, and limitations on the title. Also specify how the seller or buyer pays or receives credits, taxes, and so on.
- Determine which party will pay the fees and put all agreements in writing.

10

CONTRACTORS—CONSTRUCT A STRATEGIC PLAN

Information is a negotiator's greatest weapon.
Victor Kiam

Too often, general contractors want to be as general as possible when it comes to their pricing, scheduling, and quality of workmanship. Most novices in real estate are at a disadvantage, having little or no knowledge about the cost to repair or build particular items.

The preparation required to negotiate with the general contractor is different than what's required to negotiate with the professionals already discussed. To strengthen your position, you need to gather data on the specific property, and don't waste time getting general information about the construction industry.

POINTS TO PREPARE IN YOUR CONTRACTOR NEGOTIATIONS

Before you begin your negotiation with a contractor who will handle renovations on your property, follow these four steps to make your relationship and your renovation project go much smoother:

1. Hire an inspector.
2. Include a "penalty and reward" clause.

3. Pay a small up-front fee.
4. Set a payment schedule.

Let's discuss each of these in detail.

Hire an Inspector

The best, most effective way to gather data on the building that you're interested in purchasing is through the expertise of an inspector. The inspector examines each and every component of the building and provides you with a formal report citing its condition and defects. The fee for inspection is rather small compared to the investment that you'll make in the property. The inspector also can be useful as you prepare for your negotiation with the general contractor.

Politely (politeness goes a long way) request that the inspector write down what he or she thinks the cost would be to repair or correct any defect found in the building. Remember, it's not the responsibility of the inspector to provide you with cost estimates for these repairs and be liable for this information. Have the inspector note estimated costs on a separate piece of paper rather than in the formal inspection report.

Make sure the inspector's list is an accurate estimate to bring that building up to an acceptable standard. Remember, inspectors don't look to make a profit on any repairs. Rather, they actually examine every component of the building. On the other hand, contractors have their own benefit in mind and may not uncover all the defects that the trained eye of an inspector would notice. That's why I recommend you use the inspector's estimates in your negotiations with the general contractor.

Include a Penalty and Reward Clause

Many responsible, professional, and honest general contractors are working in the United States. However, you likely know someone who has had a bad experience working with a contractor. Most often, these bad experiences are due to poor negotiating or no negotiations at all.

Building owners get burned from general contractors usually for one or more of the following reasons:

- The job was not completed on time.
- The job went over budget.
- The contractor never finished the job.
- The quality fell below what was expected.

Your negotiations with general contractors should include obtaining a fair price for services, but it's equally important to be sure the problems noted above don't occur. To keep general contractors on the straight and narrow, I recommend you include a "penalty and reward" clause in your contract. That means if the contractor fails to complete the job on time or doesn't stay within budget, you have the right to penalize the contractor by reducing the fee. On the other hand, if the work is completed according to the contract, you can make sure the contractor receives a bonus. Again, I highly recommend you put your agreements with general contractors in writing, including the "penalty and reward" clause.

Pay a Small Up-Front Fee

In the contract, include how much money you're willing to pay up front to get the job started. Of course, you want to negotiate the smallest amount of retainer possible to get the contractor going. When you pay an up-front fee, you in effect become the bank, giving the contractor money to manage his or her cash flow—money the contractor might use on other jobs. So, keep this amount as low as possible, say 15 to 20 percent of the estimated full fee.

Set a Payment Schedule

Let's walk through the payment schedule for a single job. For example, on a $20,000 project that has a 20 percent retainer, when you assess that 25 percent of the job has been completed, then you owe the contractor $5,000. But make it your strategy to hold back 20 percent of that ($1,000), paying only $4,000 at that point in time, with the three remaining payments made at 25 percent completion intervals. In negotiations, the principle is to stay ahead of the contractor even though the contractor will try to get ahead of you. Of course, at the end of the project, you still owe $4,000. But because a contractor makes a 20 to 30 percent profit on the job, where is the profit found? In the last payment. Everything you've paid before that actually covers supplies and labor, not profit. Do you see why it's a good negotiation tactic to pay as little as you can up front to ensure the contractors you hire do a good job? Then, with the last payment, they receive their profit and, if they meet the bonus criteria, they also receive a bonus. If a contractor did an exceptionally good job, you might consider adding another $1,000 to build loyalty for your next project.

PARALLEL NEGOTIATIONS

Have you ever noticed someone staying calm, cool, and collected during a negotiation? It's refreshing to watch people serenely and methodically negotiate a transaction so that each party leaves the table feeling satisfied. It truly is an art. You may not realize, though, that one reason skilled negotiators can perform so well under difficult circumstances is that they have parallel negotiations under way.

Simply defined, a parallel negotiation strategy is negotiating with more than one entity at the same time. As a result, each advancement or retreat in the negotiation is determined by the agreements reached in the other negotiations. I think using parallel negotiations is ideal when negotiating with general contractors. Although you can't choose your opponent in every situation, with general contractors, you are in a position to select the people you will negotiate with. You are in a position of control—which helps you stay cool and calm.

*C*ome to the *T*able!

Use a Matrix to Monitor Negotiations

To successfully monitor and track negotiations, I recommend using a matrix similar to this one to help you compare the data you collect from general contractors.

CONTRACTOR	A	B	C
License number			
Cost estimate			
Project duration			
Up-front fee			
Payment schedule			
Progress reports			
Retainage			
Number of referrals			
Guarantees			
Change order procedure			
Three-day cancellation			
Insurance			
Outstanding liens			

Here is an example of a completed parallel negotiations matrix for selecting a contractor.

CONTRACTOR	A	B	C
License number	023678	Not licensed	467389
Cost estimate	$25,000	$19,000	$20,000
Project duration	3 months	2 months	Cannot determine
Up-front fee	$3,000	$4,000	$2,000
Payment schedule	3 payments	3 payments	3 payments
Progress reports	Will provide	Will not provide	Will provide
Retainage	10%	5%	10%
Number of referrals	2	5	3
Guarantees	1 year	None	None
Change order procedure	Fully explained	None	None
Three-day cancellation	No	No	Yes
Insurance	Yes	No	Yes
Outstanding liens	Yes	Yes	No

USING A CONTRACTOR AS A NEGOTIATING TOOL

Once you've negotiated your terms with a contractor, put that person to work negotiating for you. People often think they have to negotiate on their own. Remember, you don't have to go to the table alone. I recommend that you bring another professional with you—your selected contractor. As a bonus, general contractors are usually big and brawny in stature, which gives them an impressive presence at the negotiation table.

Perhaps a sticking point in your negotiation is the condition of the property and the repairs it needs. A poor condition gives you ammunition to negotiate the price as low as possible. When you get to the point in the negotiation of discussing repairs, turn it over to the expert you've brought to the table. By doing so, you've just paved the way for a string of indisputables!

Think of it this way: If you have no experience as a general contractor and neither does the seller, you'd argue over the required repairs. Or, worse, if you get caught trying to appear knowledgeable about something you know little to nothing about, you risk destroying your credibility. That's why you bring an expert with you. Make sure the contractor you select is licensed and will be recognized as an authority so that person has credibility in the negotiation, too.

Engineers or inspectors you select can be used in the same way as contractors. Your goal is to have an expert whose word is indisputable at your side. Inexperience can't argue with experience. So bring to the table professionals who will be your allies.

SUMMARY POINTS FOR CHAPTER 10: CONTRACTORS—CONSTRUCT A STRATEGIC PLAN

- To make your renovation project go much smoother, hire an inspector, include a "penalty and reward" clause, pay a small upfront fee, and set a payment schedule.
- Using parallel negotiations (talking with several contractors at once) is ideal when selecting a general contractor with whom to work.

- If the condition of the property and the repairs it needs is a sticky point in your negotiations with the seller, bring the contractor you've selected to the table and turn to this expert when discussing the cost of repairs.

11

PROPERTY MANAGERS—WATCH FOR DIFFERING GOALS

*The greatest things in the world have been done by those who
systematized their work and organized their time.*

Orison Swett Marden

In certain instances, you may wish to use a property manager to manage your real estate holdings. Property managers can be paid by a percentage of the gross revenue that the building produces and/or a flat fee. Realize that a property manager's motivation and goals differ from those of other professionals discussed. Specifically, property management firms will negotiate hard for the highest fee possible while having the fewest number of responsibilities— all under the auspices of a long-term, guaranteed contract.

SETTING FEES WITH PROPERTY MANAGERS

Property management services are extremely varied, with no set contract for all property managers to use. You can have a property manager do as little or as much as you'd like. Of course, property managers will seek the highest fee for their services, no matter how much they do. These fees vary from 3 to 5 percent of the gross income of a property, and they also vary in different parts of the country.

I suggest that in your negotiation with property managers you spell out your fee agreements explicitly. Fees should be a percentage of the gross income that's actually collected, not the gross income that is projected. In addition, payment for all services provided should be tied to specific performance measurements. For example, the property manager should be obligated to forward a detailed periodic report to you and should maintain a minimum level of occupancy in the building. The manager also could be required to keep the utility costs within a certain acceptable range. You can be as creative as possible with these requirements, but be sure to make them. Add all the items you need to be managed as an addendum to the basic contract right from the beginning. Negotiate as many responsibilities as possible. This will clearly reduce any confusion about what is expected.

Set it up so that your property managers receive a reduced percentage of the gross income if they fail to achieve one or more of the performance measurements you've spelled out as an addition to the basic contract. Most property managers will resist this type of addition. However, the confident, experienced ones will accept this requirement or work out a compromise with you.

LONG-TERM CONTRACTS

Naturally, property managers seek to sign long-term contracts that assure them of a steady stream of income over a long time. Similar to the contract that you may have with a real estate broker, be sure to negotiate in an escape clause. That means that if a property manager fails to live up to his or her responsibilities fully or doesn't meet one or more of the performance measurements, then you have the option to immediately terminate the contract. (See Appendix D for a sample Real Estate Management Contract.)

SUMMARY POINTS FOR CHAPTER 11: PROPERTY MANAGERS—WATCH FOR DIFFERING GOALS

- Make fees for property managers a percentage of the gross income that's actually collected, not the gross income that is projected.
- Tie payment for services provided to specific performance measurements.
- When setting up a contract with a property manager or property management company, be sure to negotiate in an escape clause.

*C*ome to the *T*able!

Foil to Foil

A foil is often described as the "fall guy." In negotiating with the property manager or any of the others involved in negotiating real estate deals, you may be negotiated into a corner or may be pressed to make a decision. The best escape strategy is the use of a foil. Some people describe it as deferring to a higher authority. The exit dialogue may go something like this: "Mike, I can understand your position. I respect that you're under a deadline and you need a decision from me. Unfortunately, I have a partner. I just can't make a unilateral decision on that issue. I need time to talk to my partner." The partner has become the foil. And here's the great part—he or she can be real or imaginary.

12

TENANTS—MARKET TO THEM WELL

Sherlock Holmes remarked to Dr. Watson: "While the individual man is an insoluble puzzle, in the aggregate, he becomes a mathematical certainty. You can never foretell what any one man will do, but you can always predict with precision what an average number of men will be up to. Individuals vary but percentages remain constant."

Sir Arthur Conan Doyle

Tenants are the source of your revenue; therefore, it's critical to market to them well. Once you have their attention, how you negotiate with them often depends on current market conditions.

Generally speaking, if there's a great deal of available space for rent in a certain market, a landlord is in a weak position to negotiate high rents, although there are exceptions to this rule. For example, if a landlord owns a unique or highly desirable space, he or she can negotiate from a position of strength.

On the flip side, if little available space exists in the market, then the landlord can be more selective and demand higher rents, because the law of supply and demand allows the landlord to negotiate from a position of strength.

SETTING UP A LONG-TERM RELATIONSHIP

Pay attention to one important difference between negotiating with a tenant and negotiating with a seller: The business relationship between a buyer and a seller is a one-time relationship focused on the purchase of a property. Most likely after you purchase the property, your relationship with the seller ends. However, with a tenant, you are negotiating a lease that sets forth the rights and obligations of both parties for a long time, sometimes as long as 15 years. Understand that your initial negotiation sets the tone of the relationship. Make it amiable and future communications will be easy.

TWO TYPES OF TENANTS: COMMERCIAL AND RESIDENTIAL

Tenants fall into two categories: commercial and residential. Negotiating with commercial tenants is often more difficult because business owners usually have more experience in real estate matters than residential tenants. In addition, negotiations with a commercial tenant are commonly more complicated. Commercial leases carry more components and have longer terms than residential leases.

Commercial Tenants

Typically, you'll negotiate against two categories of commercial tenants: office tenants, who lease space on the second floor and up in a commercial or mixed-use building, or retail tenants, who lease the ground floor areas of your property. Typical retail tenants are dry-use retail tenants, which means they don't require water. They include apparel stores, office-supply stores, shoe stores, and so on. Commercial buildings also have wet-use retail tenants, such as restaurants, salons, delicatessens, and more.

Commercial real estate lease. For commercial tenants, you'll want to negotiate a substantial security deposit, certainly enough to cover the following:

- Two months of rent
- The amount of the free rent
- Any construction or repair money you spend
- Brokerage fees to transact the deal
- Legal fees related to the deal

For example, I'm negotiating with an office tenant for a 5,000-square-foot office space in New York City at $36 per square foot. The rent is $15,000 a month, the brokerage fee is $64,800, and I need to spend $10,000 to refurbish the place before the tenant can move in. In addition, legal fees to handle this transaction will cost approximately $5,000 and I have agreed to give the new tenant one month of rent free. Therefore, I would calculate the security deposit as follows:

Two months of rent	$30,000
One month of free rent	15,000
Refurbish	10,000
Broker fees	64,800
Legal fees	5,000
Security deposit	$124,800

Of course, this is a logical approach to negotiating the security deposit amount, but I still haven't factored in market conditions. If it is a tenants' market, I'd have to be more willing to reduce the amount of the security deposit to close this deal. If it is a strong landlord's market and I have many tenants to choose from all vying for my space, I should be able to follow the calculations above. If the commercial tenant is rated as a AAA company with strong financial strength, it may be prudent to negotiate a lower security deposit to obtain a quality tenant.

Subleasing and assignment. The subleasing clause in a commercial real estate lease can be heavily negotiated. The key negotiating points to keep in mind are profits and financial tests.

If you allow your tenants to sublease or assign the space to another party, include language in the lease stating that if the tenant leases the space to a subtenant for a greater rent amount, then *you* are entitled to the profit, not the tenant. The negotiation logic in this situation is to explain to the tenants that *you* are in the real estate business and that *they* are not. Therefore, you should be the beneficiary of any profits derived from the sublet.

It's important that the subtenant be financially strong and ideally even stronger financially than the initial tenant. To ensure that you are getting a good subtenant, negotiate into the sublease clause that the subtenant must undergo a financial test. Included on this financial test would be the following:

- Subtenant's net worth must be equal to or greater than the existing tenant's.
- Subtenant must be willing to pay two months of extra security deposit than is already held in escrow.

Another "test" you could add to the clause is that the owner of the subtenant company must have at least ten years of experience in managing such a company and, if it's a retail tenant, that the subtenant operates a similar business and will have price points similar to the existing tenant's.

Good Guy Guarantee

In dealing with commercial tenants, especially retail tenants, it may be beneficial to include a Good Guy Guarantee, which is actually a limited liability clause. (See Appendix E for a sample Good Guy Guarantee form.) When retailers, especially restaurants, face financial difficulty, they may stop paying rent and yet still remain in the space. They often stay for months while the landlord fights them in court and tries to evict them. It also may be necessary for the landlord to visit them while they are operating their business, which could disturb the customers. The situation can quickly grow ugly.

The Good Guy Guarantee is basically an agreement between a tenant and a landlord to act like "good guys." For example, store owners would use it as a guarantee to give the landlord notice if they have financial difficulty. It could mean giving up their rights to a trial by jury, promising to pay all back rent due, and handing over the keys peacefully. The landlord then promises that the tenants won't have to pay future rent (that is, pay rent after the day the tenants surrender the space).

Keep in mind that in a standard lease, the tenants owe all the rent due whether they occupy the space or not. For example, if a tenant signs a ten-year lease and occupies the space for two years then decides to close the business, that tenant still owes the landlord rent to cover eight years.

The good news about preparing a negotiation with a commercial tenant concerns the research. You'll find it's easier to access more in-depth information regarding the commercial market than the residential market.

Residential Tenants

The components of the negotiation with residential tenants are few, and they are less technical than for commercial tenants. The most important points to consider follow.

Lease term. It is customary for residential leases to be for a length of one year or perhaps two. If your property is in a good economy with rents rising and forecast to continue to rise, ideally you want the term of your residential leases to be as short as possible so you can raise the amount of rent. However, if your property is in a flat economy, it's apparent that rents should stay the same or decrease slightly so you can lock in a good tenant with a two-year lease.

Rent. One of the most difficult challenges is to negotiate the highest rent possible—which in effect is the highest rent the market will bear. The sidebar on the next page provides an example of how I used marketplace trends to achieve the highest rent for a specific property.

Restoration clause. This clause, like the restoration clause in a commercial lease (which we'll get to shortly), is very powerful. I suggest you negotiate into the residential lease that the tenants will be required to restore the apartment to the exact condition in which it was first rented to them.

Security deposits. Landlord-tenant courts have been inundated with litigations between landlords and tenants. Quite often it takes months to achieve a settlement. Therefore, it's important to negotiate a substantial but reasonable amount for a security deposit. I think that securing an amount to cover only one month's or two months' rent is not sufficient. I recommend asking for a three-month security deposit, plus the first month's rent.

Use Marketplace Trends to Set Rent

I was interested in buying a classic four-story, four-apartment brownstone in New York City. One that was vacant had just come on the market as part of an estate sale. The house had been built in 1865 and the 90-year-old deceased gentleman had lived in this house for his entire life. The brownstone building itself and the antique furniture that came with it was full of exquisite detail.

In considering my purchase, I was having difficulty calculating the potential rental income for this property because I wasn't sure how much I could obtain through negotiation with future tenants. I asked the real estate broker selling the building if he would let me borrow a set of keys and show one of the four apartments to a few potential residential tenants. I assured the broker that I was sincerely interested in buying the place, but I was unsure of its rental potential.

My next step was to place an ad in the paper, citing the rent at "$1,500 a month or best offer." I immediately received 41 responses. When people called, I told them up front that I would probably buy the building but was still in negotiation. Then I scheduled appointments with the first ten people who had called.

The first people who came told me they would be interested in renting the apartment for $1,500 if and when I bought the building. The next person who came also liked the apartment. I asked him if he would be willing to pay $1,600. He said, "Yes, most certainly," and wished me luck in the purchase of the building. With every new prospect, I raised the asking price on the rent.

When talking with potential renters, I wrote down each person's name, telephone number, and the stated (and agreed on) rent amount. I did this with each person who came by until one gentleman told me that I was crazy to be asking $2,100 a month. He absolutely wouldn't pay it! I knew then that the market rent I could command was $2,000. Next, I recalculated my income and expense projections, and was satisfied with the result. I then called the real estate broker and negotiated the price and conditions. When I bought the property 60 days later, I had each of the prospective tenants' names and numbers in hand. A week after I bought the building, I succeeded in renting each apartment at $2,000 a month.

Avoid coterminous. Terms that expire at the same day are called "coterminous." That means if you have more than one tenant in your building, avoid having some or all of your tenants' leases expiring the same month if you possibly can. In the event that two or more of your tenants' leases expire the same month, it's possible they may simultaneously choose not to renew and end up vacating the building. This could put undue financial pressure on you, especially if you can't find replacement tenants quickly.

Occupant limits. Apartments are designed to accommodate only a certain number of occupants. Often a landlord will forget to include some kind of clause that limits the number of people who can actually live in an apartment. Be sure to negotiate a clause that specifically states how many people are allowed to live in your rental unit.

KEY NEGOTIATION POINTS FOR COMMERCIAL TENANTS

A negotiation with commercial tenants will cover many points. You want to negotiate the following basic elements to create the Terms and Conditions sheet:

- Base rent
- Term of lease
- Lease commencement date
- Rent commencement date
- Operating escalations
- Real estate tax
- Security deposit
- Construction work prior to the move in
- Subleasing and assignments

These make up the key components of the lease that are important to become familiar with.

Keep in mind that when you negotiate with a tenant, it's assumed you'll be using your real estate broker as your ally in the negotiations. In fact, some real estate investors and building owners rely completely on their brokers to handle the transactions. I suggest that you accompany your real estate broker to all of the negotiation meetings. Most professional commercial real estate brokers welcome the owner's participation at key meetings because decisions can be made quickly when the owner is present. However, it's important that you collaborate with your broker to determine the negotiation tactics you'll use. You may decide that at times your presence would be a detriment. It all depends on the goal you've set for that particular negotiation session.

CREATE A STANDARD LEASE

As the owner of the property, you can simplify and strengthen your negotiation position by creating a customized form of lease that becomes your standard lease. The standard form of lease that can be purchased at a stationery store is not sufficient to protect you; however, you can use it as a boilerplate when creating your own. You and your lawyer should discuss the lease components noted earlier in this chapter and draft an addendum to the boilerplate lease to make it part of your customized lease.

Pay attention to the following clauses that are important to negotiate into your lease proposal and eventually into the lease itself:

- "Use" clause
- Term of the lease
- "Operating escalation" clause
- "Kick out" and "right to audit" clauses
- Restoration clause

"Use" Clause

The "use" clause should be as specific as possible to prevent a tenant from easily subleasing or assigning the lease. A strict use clause means that the tenant only can sublease to a subtenant in that specific use category. For example, if the lease merely said "for retail use," then the tenant could sublease the space for any type of retail use. If the use clause was more specific—for example, it cited, "space to be used as a high-end shoe store"—then the tenant would only be allowed to sublease the space to a high-end shoe store. This clearly puts the tenant at a disadvantage when approaching the landlord to request and negotiate a sublease.

Term of the Lease

In a real estate market that's characterized by rising rents, landlords are better off negotiating short-term leases so they can ratchet up the rents each time a lease needs to be renewed. In most major U.S. cities, a short-term lease is typically one that lasts one to three years, four- to seven-year leases are considered medium-term leases, and eight years and above are considered long-term leases. Conversely, in a real estate market in which rents are dropping, it may be in the best interest of the landlord to negotiate a long-term lease and lock in a rate that will be above market for quite some time.

"Operating Escalation" Clause

The basic idea behind an operating escalation clause is to provide landlords with extra income so they can cover the increase in their operating expenses (the expenses necessary to operate and maintain the building). There are several ways to incorporate an operating escalation clause into a lease.

In an economy with increasing interest rates, it's more advantageous for a landlord to negotiate into the lease a consumer price index (CPI) operating escalation. The CPI communicates monthly data on changes in the prices paid by urban consumers for a representative basket of goods and services.

Consumer price index escalation, which is applied to the rents every year, is cumulative. For example, if the CPI is 3.5 percent, then the tenant's rent for that particular year would increase by 3.5 percent. If the CPI for the following year is 5 percent, the tenant's rent would also increase by 5 percent.

The second operating escalation that can be negotiated into the lease is a straight percentage increase escalation. In this case, the landlord and tenant negotiate a flat percent increase to be applied each year over the course of the lease term. For example, if a 3 percent increase is applied annually, the landlord makes it clear ahead of time that the tenant's rent would increase by 3 percent each year.

"Kick Out" and "Right to Audit" Clauses

A kick out clause is negotiated into leases for tenants operating retail businesses. As a basic concept, the landlord and the tenant agree that the tenant must achieve a particular gross income each year. If the tenant does *not* achieve the gross income figure, the landlord has the right to kick out the tenant.

Along with the kick out clause, the landlord needs to negotiate a right to audit clause. This gives the landlord the right to review for accuracy the gross income figures being reported from the tenant to the landlord.

Restoration Clause

An important clause to negotiate into the tenant's lease is the restoration clause, an often-overlooked clause that gives the landlord an advantage during the negotiation for renewing the lease.

At the end of the lease, contention often takes place between the landlord and tenant to determine if the security deposit should be returned. The restoration clause basically states that the tenant must return the space back to its original condition. That means if the tenants added carpet, painted the walls, and improved the lighting fixtures, they'd be required to remove the carpeting, paint the walls back to the original color, and reinstall the original light fixtures. Tenants realize it's too costly to restore the property to its original condition, so they let the landlord keep all or a part of the security deposit in lieu of complying with the stated restoration clause.

WALKING THROUGH A TENANT NEGOTIATION

It is important to obtain information about the financial status of your tenants, whether an individual or a company, so you know who you are dealing with. Early on in the negotiation, ask them to fill out a financial statement form. (See Appendix F for a sample financial statement form.)

A negotiation with a commercial real estate tenant starts with a proposal. The market itself dictates who should send the first proposal. For example, if it's a strong landlord's market in which space is tight, you should request that the tenant send you an offer to lease space.

To accelerate the negotiation and help you analyze multiple proposals sent from other prospective tenants, it's helpful to request that the proposal be sent in a particular format. (You may want to send prospective tenants a blank proposal form that outlines the lease components and the order of the components.) This procedure gives you some strength in the negotiation because you are setting the agenda on what items will be included and what items will not.

Figure 12.1 is a typical proposal for the leasing of an office space.

THE FIVE-COLUMN METHOD

The greatest negotiators—generals, emperors, politicians, CEOs—all use a plan to conduct their negotiations. In fact, many of them play out probable conversations as a way to practice a pending negotiation and imagine how it will proceed (see Chapter 15 for more on role-playing).

I have been involved in thousands of real estate negotiations. Early on in my career, I created a method to project the outcome of and keep track of advances in my negotiation. I refer to that method as the Five Column Method. It's a visual device that can help anyone develop a strong negotiation plan.

In the Five Column Method, you devise a matrix in which the center is marked as the "strike"—the deal you think will really happen. Whatever you're negotiating for, list the elements on the left. The elements of the strike are the road map of where you're going—the values in the deal that you'll accept. After you've done as much research as you can, you'll have a gut feeling of where it's going to go.

The Five Column Method features six proposal phases, because I find that's what it takes in the real estate world. If it goes to more than six steps, something is inherently wrong with the deal and this particular deal gets lost in other deals. If the process goes too fast, with fewer than

FIGURE 12.1 *Sample Lease Proposal*

(Company letterhead)

Mr. John Smith
Title
Company
Address
City, State, Zip code

Re: The leasing of the second floor at 100 Main Street

Dear Mr. Smith:

Our customer, United States Financial Company, currently located at 500 Fifth Avenue, has authorized us to submit the following proposal:

Building:	100 Main Street
Space:	Entire third floor
Area:	10,000 square feet
Use:	General, administrative, and executive offices
Term:	10 years
Rent:	Years 1 to 5 $30 per square foot
	Years 6 to 10 $35 per square foot
Possession and lease commencement:	May 1, 2005
Rent commencement:	August 1, 2005
Landlord's work:	Landlord will paint the premises, upgrade the bathrooms, relamp the lights, and replace the carpet.
Security deposit:	$90,000
Electricity:	$3.00 per square foot
Operating escalations:	3 percent per year
Tax escalations:	Increase in real estate taxes above the base fiscal year 2005/2006.
Subleasing and assignment:	Tenant shall have the right to assign or sublease any portion, or the entire premises, upon written consent of landlord, not to be unreasonably withheld. Tenant may assign or sublease the premises to any and all affiliates without the landlord's consent.
Cleaning:	Standard office cleaning will be included in the base rental.
Brokerage:	Landlord shall pay the broker one full commission.

This proposal is submitted to you in strict confidence for negotiation purposes only. It is subject to final review and approval of tenant and its Board of Directors. We look forward to your favorable response and assure you of our full cooperation.

Very truly yours,

George F. Donohue

Accepted by: _____ as of this date: _____

Source: © George F. Donohue

six steps, it could mean you're paying too much money or accepting too little. These rounds provide a volley of exchanges that seem to work well.

My method uses the following chart.

First, determine what your strike deal is, then write in the values you will finally accept in the center column.

DEAL	1st	3rd	STRIKE	4th	2nd
Rent			$30/sq. ft.		
Free rent			3 months		
Term			7 years		
Security deposit			4 months		

The second step is to fill in the first column with the elements you will propose first.

DEAL	1st	3rd	STRIKE	4th	2nd
Rent	$26		$30/sq. ft.		
Free rent	6		3 months		
Term	15		7 years		
Security deposit	0		4 months		

The third step is to fill in the column cited as "2nd"—your educated guess on what your opponents will counteroffer.

DEAL	1st	3rd	STRIKE	4th	2nd
Rent	$26		$30/sq. ft.		$28
Free rent	6		3 months		1
Term	15		7 years		5
Security deposit	0		4 months		6

The fourth step is to enter under the column designated as "3rd" what your counteroffer will be to your opponents' first counteroffer.

DEAL	1st	3rd	STRIKE	4th	2nd
Rent	$26	$28.50	$30/sq. ft		$28
Free rent	6	5	3 months		1
Term	15	10	7 years		5
Security deposit	0	1	4 months		6

The fifth step is to enter what you believe to be the opposing party's subsequent response.

DEAL	1st	3rd	STRIKE	4th	2nd
Rent	$26	$28.50	$30/sq. ft.	$29.50	$28
Free rent	6	5	3 months	2	1
Term	15	10	7 years	5	5
Security deposit	0	1	4 months	5	6

The Final Step

In the final step, which is the most important, you examine the last table and go through the sequence of offers and counteroffers to determine if it is a reasonable, believable, sequence of proposals back and forth. Your goal is to script out each step along the way. If, after you examine the last table, you decide that one of the proposals may be off, go back and revise the values in that particular column.

Using the Five Column Method

The Five Column Method takes you through the entire negotiation process using the various tables. Remember, these tables are for your eyes only. After each round of negotiation, refer back to them to see how close you progressed in the deal compared with your predictions.

If you find you're doing well in your negotiations and achieving better results than you predicted, stay the course and make the best of them. However, if you're falling behind compared to the scripted plan, then look carefully at the sequence of events again and modify your offers appropriately.

SUMMARY POINTS FOR CHAPTER 12: TENANTS—MARKET TO THEM WELL

- Remember that, with a tenant, you are negotiating a lease that sets forth the rights and obligations of both parties for a long time. It's not a short-term relationship.

- Commercial leases carry more components and have longer terms than residential leases.
- When determining the amount of security deposit to charge commercial tenants, take into account market conditions as well as specific costs.
- When you want to limit liability issues with your commercial tenants, incorporate a Good Guy Guarantee clause (see Appendix E) into the contract.
- Key components of a commercial lease include base rent, term of the lease, lease commencement date, rent commencement date, operating escalations, real estate tax, security deposit, construction work prior to the move in, plus subleasing and assignments.
- Pay attention to negotiating certain clauses into your lease proposal and eventually into the lease itself. They include a use clause, term of lease, operating escalation clause, kick out and right to audit clauses, and restoration clause.
- Be sure to obtain information about the financial status of your tenants, whether an individual or a company, to verify their ability to pay.
- Use a Five Column Method, using a matrix in which the center is marked as the "strike"—the deal you think will really happen—as an effective negotiation tool.

13

BUYERS—TAKING THE DRIVER'S SEAT

Let us never negotiate out of fear. But let us never fear to negotiate.

John F. Kennedy

Real estate moves in cycles. In a period of "irrational exuberance"—to use Federal Reserve Chairman Alan Greenspan's phrase—the values of real estate may be artificial or inflated, thus protecting poor negotiators from their lack of negotiating skills. Some people enter the business of real estate investing in the beginning of an upward cycle and enjoy a few years watching real estate values increase. This early success could be misleading to others and cause them to be ill prepared for future negotiations.

When the market turns and values begin to slide, real estate buyers have the advantage over sellers. If you are a seller or representing a seller in a downward market, you can apply many of the tips and techniques already described in this book and negotiate well. But I'd like to emphasize several important considerations in negotiating against buyers when market conditions are tough.

VULTURE BUYERS

During a strong downward cycle, a particular kind of buyer surfaces—the "vulture buyer" or "opportunity buyer." Sellers need to be able to identify from the onset the type of buyer that is approaching them, especially the vulture buyers.

Some people characterize vulture buyers as bottom feeders. They can be one individual, a small group of buyers banded together, or a large, organized enterprise. They usually seek to buy properties from owners who are already in a distressed situation (for example, sellers who are having difficulty paying the mortgage and/or other expenses due to a death, divorce, relocation, etc.). These buyers usually have ready cash and can move quickly. They seek heavily discounted prices and only will pay well below market prices.

To protect themselves from vulture or opportunity buyers, sellers need to be cautious and not reveal that they're experiencing financial hemorrhaging. These buyers may try to tie up the property or purposefully slow-peddle the deal to press sellers further into bankruptcy or to cause them to resort to having a fire sale.

NEGOTIATING REAL ESTATE BUBBLES

The key to successfully negotiating the real estate bubble is preparation—remember the Coast Guard's motto: Semper Paratus (Always Prepared). If a real estate market bubble appears to be poised to burst, it's time to set your plan in motion. What are your indicators? For one, the real estate market bubble may be ready to burst if every major financial publication starts carrying prominent stories of warning. For example, if Federal Reserve Chairman Alan Greenspan publicly discusses interest rate increases or actually begins to ratchet rates up, this could be a sign that the investment bubble is ready to burst.

When the values start to trend downward and you need or want to sell, prepare for your negotiations by following the five critical steps that are detailed next.

Step One: Get Your Property Appraised

Get a handle on what your property is truly worth. Spend a few dollars and have two or three separate appraisers evaluate your property. Be realistic and honest with yourself. In a downward-trending market, the appraised prices could be the most you could ever get for the property in the near future. Remember, it takes 30 to 90 days to close on a deal. So don't fall in love with the appraisals, because you may be chasing a runaway train. The longer you hold on to an inflated price in a down market, the more likely you'll end up selling at a steep discount.

Step Two: Convert an Adjustable Rate Mortgage to a Fixed Rate Mortgage

If you have an adjustable rate mortgage (ARM), arrange to convert that mortgage into a fixed rate and an assumable mortgage. This may cost a few dollars but it will be well worth the trouble because it will provide you with leverage in your negotiating position. If you can offer a potential buyer your property along with an assumable mortgage at a low fixed rate, it will make your property more attractive to buyers than other similar properties.

Step Three: Be Prepared to "Take Back Paper"

The expression "take back paper" means to provide financing to the buyer of your property. This will greatly help the buyer who may be willing to pay your price but only can obtain a limited portion of the mortgage from a financial lender.

For example, let's say your property is appraised at $300,000 and prices are starting to fall. A potential buyer is interested in paying $275,000 for the property, but the buyer only can get a $190,000 mortgage and has $55,000 in cash for a down payment. The $55,000 is 20 percent of $245,000 ($55,000 down plus a $190,000 mortgage equals $245,000). The buyer is still short $30,000 to purchase the property.

The solution could be for your lawyer and the buyer's lawyer to draw up a promissory note or loan document for $30,000 to be paid back over five years. You'll receive the $245,000 at closing and then a payment of approximately $500 per month for five years.

The knee-jerk alternative is to find the buyers who are willing to pay full price without the complication of a promissory note or additional financing. However, finding this type of buyer in a real estate market in which the bubble is bursting could take time—one month, two months, six months, or perhaps even longer.

Another alternative is to tell potential buyers to seek another bank and hope they can find one that will lend them the full amount. But this too could take quite some time—from one to three months. Remember, in a downward-trending market, the amount of time you spend delaying could cost you thousands of dollars.

Step Four: Include Your Bottom-Line Price and Last Closing Date in Your Broker's Contract

If you retain a real estate broker to sell your property, explicitly negotiate for your bottom-line price and a drop-dead closing date. In other words, negotiate into the brokerage agreement that the broker will find a buyer who will pay no less than X amount of dollars and will have a contract of sale signed by a certain date with the closing date on or before a specific date.

Step Five: Build a Matrix of Comparables

Science tells us that the bursting of a real bubble is preceded by increased surface tension of the sphere. In the preburst days of a real estate market, that tension will increase and you'll feel it. In the meantime, create a matrix of comparables, similar to the one in Figure 13.1, and validate it often.

The first step in building your matrix is to have your real estate broker select eight to ten other properties currently on the market that are similar to your building and in proximity to your property, but they don't need to be exactly like your property. The most important item you'll be tracking in the matrix of comparables is the weekly percentage changes in the prices of the comparable properties.

FIGURE 13.1 *Matrix of Comparables*

Address	Contact	Phone	Price on 3/1	Price on 3/8	Diff.	Price on 3/15	Price on 3/22	Diff.
100 Main St.	R. Jones	555-555-1111	$300,000	$285,000	–5%	$285,000	$271,000	–5%
120 Main St.	S. Day	555-555-2222	$290,000	$270,000				
130 Main St.	T. Small	555-555-3333	$310,000	$298,000	–4%			
Your home			$315,000					

Source: © George F. Donohue

Every week, track each of the buildings listed in your matrix. You can do this by asking your real estate broker for the updated data and then validating the information by calling the real estate broker who represents each specific property. Each week, calculate the drop in price, if any.

For example, a property that first priced at $300,000 then dropped to $285,000 reflects a 5 percent drop:

$300,000 – $285,000 = $15,000, and $15,000 ÷ $300,000 = 5 percent.

If the majority of the asking prices of the properties are declining, strongly consider repricing your property in line with or slightly below the others, assuming you need to sell quickly.

In a euphoric upward-trending real estate market, few property owners conduct this type of analysis. Many of them gloat in their seemingly good fortune, sometimes not aware of how much money they've left on the table. However, in a time when talk turns to bubble bursting, it's critical to behave like a weekly price watchdog. Monitoring this chart will help you do that, and it will become an important aid in all of your negotiations.

THINKING OUTSIDE THE BOX

You've likely heard the expression "thinking outside the box," but how can thinking outside the box help you at the negotiation table?

The "box" is thought of as the traditional business environment that a seller and buyer negotiate within. Thinking "outside the box" is

Solving a Seller's Dilemma

A seller and buyer were in negotiations for a two-family home. The seller was not under duress to sell the property; he genuinely wanted to sell the property at his stated price. The buyer had the financial ability to purchase the property and was genuinely interested in it as an investment. The buyer had lined up alternative choices in the same price range and quality, but he preferred this particular property.

The buyer and seller engaged in negotiations for quite some time, but couldn't come to an agreement on the price—the price difference still fell $20,000 apart. Given that this two-family home was $350,000, it seemed that the $20,000 gap could be closed. To an outsider, the apparent solution might be to split the difference—the buyer paying $10,000 more than he would like and the seller receiving $10,000 less than he would like.

But in this case, the seller was stubborn; he wanted no less than $350,000. The buyer tried every negotiating tactic he knew to reduce the price to $330,000. Before long, though, something that happens when two people negotiate in good faith occurred—the two gentlemen became friendly. Finally, in frustration, the buyer asked the seller point-blank, "Why will you not reduce the price from $350,000 to $330,000?" The seller, believing that he could confide in the buyer, explained that he had a daughter in college who had an outstanding tuition bill of $20,000. If he sold the property for $330,000, he wouldn't have enough profit to pay off the student loan and cover the tuition bill as a gift to his daughter. After that conversation, the buyer understood the seller's situation more clearly and respected his position.

Then the two men began to think outside the box. In a moment of brainstorming, the buyer asked the seller if the student loan was assignable, meaning was it possible for the buyer to assume the loan from his daughter? A light bulb went on. The seller called the bank and found out that the loan properties did indeed allow someone else to take it over. It was the perfect solution. They set it up so that the buyer began paying off the loan and they agreed that the seller didn't have to.

If you ever feel you've come to an impasse in a negotiation and believe the other party is trying in good faith to close the deal, suggest that the two of you sit down and think collaboratively outside the box to explore alternative solutions.

What Can the Other Side Give That You Want?

I was involved in an important negotiation regarding a major office lease transaction with a well-known international publishing company.

At the time, we were desperately seeking office tenants and the market didn't favor us. In this tenants' market, landlords were competing aggressively, especially for well-known, financially strong office tenants. Millions of dollars of much-needed revenue was at stake.

Our negotiation team consisted of my senior officer and me. On the other side were representatives of the publishing company—the publisher, his real estate representative, his corporate lawyer, and a few middle-management people. The negotiation had dragged on for two months and, as we sat down to discuss the final items, we were still dollars apart on the rental rate. We needed to achieve a certain minimum rate to make the lease transaction profitable, and we knew our Board would not let us go below that rental number. The publishing company, which had been operating for more than 100 years and was well known for its international news coverage, also had a tight budget. The decision makers could not increase their offer.

I distinctly remember a moment when we were all sitting at a huge conference table and a long silence hung heavy in the room. No one was willing to budge nor could anyone come up with a solution to close the gap.

I knew that we had to obtain a particular rent level because our expenses were quite high, so I started to mentally go through the list of expenses burdening us: electricity, labor, other operating expenses, marketing, and advertising.

That's when a light bulb went off!

I leaned over to my senior officer, covered my mouth, and whispered in his ear, "I think we can get them to pay for all of our advertising expenses."

My negotiation partner could see exactly where I was going with that statement. We both knew that this international publication was an excellent publication in which to market our building complex. But it was extremely costly for us to run ads in their publication. However, for the decision makers, their advertising was just another space in their large publication. It wasn't a true dollar expense for them to "give" us advertising.

My senior officer looked at me and said, "Try it."

I broke the silence, leaned forward, and said, "Gentlemen, it looks as though we are at a stalemate. However, I would like to request that you patronize me with an idea that may be beneficial to both of us. It is slightly unorthodox but I think it might work.

"One of our costliest expenses is marketing and advertising. If you could help us in regard to this item, I think we can close the gap. Are you willing and able to give us free advertising for a decent duration of time?"

The publisher smiled. He knew we had found a solution. It was something that they could easily provide. So we calculated what the gap was, then wrote a clause into our agreement that they would provide us with advertising equal to the value of the gap.

Always probe and ask about what items could be used to close the gap—other than money or real estate property. Find a win-win, "out of the box" solution.

the ability to look beyond the property, the mortgage, the price, the closing date, and all the components. In short, it means looking beyond the ordinary.

WHAT ABOUT DEADLINES?

Deadlines always make negotiations difficult. If you are selling a property by a certain fixed deadline and negotiating against a buyer who has no time constraints, you are at a distinct disadvantage. So in your negotiations, I suggest you never reveal your actual deadline to your opponent.

Usually sellers are strapped with a deadline when an unusual occurrence happens in their lives. For example, a seller may need to quickly dispose of his property if he's in the middle of a divorce, or if he has been told by his employer that he will be relocating soon to another city, or if he lost his job and may not be able to pay the mortgage. In fact, life events like these often precipitate putting a property on the market and selling it quickly.

Touché in Taipei

I learned about deadlines and negotiating real estate the hard way when I was visiting Taiwan to complete a real estate deal. I'd planned to spend two weeks in the city of Taipei negotiating the deal. In my mind, that seemed like a sufficient amount of time to execute an agreement that had already outlined the basic terms and conditions of the deal.

When picking me up from the airport, the representative from the other party asked me how long I was staying in Taipei. (Keep in mind, I had just spent the past 20 hours on an airplane from New York to Taiwan.) I quickly and inadvertently told him I was staying for two weeks, then I spelled out the exact date and time I was leaving Taipei.

I had forgotten all about his question the next day when I contacted the other party to begin the deal making. During those two weeks, very little happened; I clearly didn't make much progress in the negotiations. All the while, my superiors in New York were asking me for progress reports. I continued to tell them I was making little progress. On the last day, the other side finally started to make its demands—aggressively and clearly. You see, they made good use of the information they'd learned about my departure date. At the negotiation table, they squeezed me right up until my deadline, putting me at a disadvantage.

I rarely make the same mistake twice. The next time I went to Asia to negotiate a real estate deal, I was asked the same question in the airport when I arrived. This time my answer was that I had an open ticket and a good number of vacation days and personal days. I really had no idea when I would have to return to New York.

CHOOSING A PLACE TO NEGOTIATE

The ideal place to negotiate a real estate deal is on your own turf because you'll likely feel stronger there, while your opponent might feel uncomfortable. If you're a seller negotiating against a buyer, I think the best place to negotiate is right at the property that's going to be purchased. It's your property (so you're on your own turf) and the buyers are surrounded by the very thing they want to acquire.

However, sometimes doing this may not be convenient if, for example, you have tenants occupying the building. In that case, I suggest you hold the negotiation in your office or your home. Another place to negotiate would be a neutral location like a quiet restaurant. The last place you want to negotiate in is in your opponent's office or home.

If you are the decision maker or negotiator for your team, pay attention to details such as choosing a round table. Make the chair setup simple. Sit across from the most senior person from the other team. Position your most trusted and knowledgeable team members to your left and right. All these details help put you in the driver's seat.

> ### Round Tables
>
> When I negotiated deals at the World Trade Center, I had several choices for reserving conference rooms, so I always chose a room that had a circular table instead of a rectangular one. The rectangular shape automatically and perhaps subliminally suggests a skirmish, while the table itself represents the scrimmage line. I noticed that I always achieved better results in the rooms that had a circular table. Everyone at a round table feels they have an equal stake in the negotiation; it's as if there is one problem everyone is trying to solve.

CREATE AN AGENDA

It's also important to bring to the negotiation meeting a printed agenda with enough copies for everyone. Some people regard the agenda preparation as insignificant, but that's a dangerous mistake to make. By writing the agenda and distributing it at the meeting, you control what subjects will be discussed and in what order. It takes a strong opponent to look at the agenda, crumple it up, and declare that there will not be an agenda. In fact, I have never seen that happen. People act like lemmings when an agenda is put in front of them. Often they're relieved that they didn't have to put it together themselves so they willingly follow along.

You want to make the agenda simple and straightforward. I suggest you spend a great deal of time and thought creating the sequence of the agenda to match your negotiation plan. Figure 13.2 is an example of a

FIGURE 13.2 Agenda

Agenda for Purchase of 100 Main Street

November 23, 2005

Attendees:
George F. Donohue
John Smith
William Jones

- Interior condition of the property
- Existing tenants
- Tax history
- Furniture
- Roof
- Down payment
- Interest rate contingency
- Price
- Closing date
- Fuel costs in winter
- Next meeting date and time

---

sample agenda to follow. What is the most important item of negotiation on this agenda?

In this example, let's say price is the most important element to you as an investor. Notice that price is not put at either the beginning or end of the agenda. Placing it at the very beginning doesn't give you a chance to feel out your opponents and shows your hand too quickly. Placing it at the very end may cause your opponents' guard to go up. Remember, because you created and distributed the agenda, it's *your* agenda. It should put you in a position of control.

When you're sitting across from your opponents, imagine an old pharmaceutical scale. During the negotiation, you each slowly put up your weights and see where you find the balance. To tip the scales in your favor, you want to see where the weights on the scale go first. If you list the price toward the end of your agenda, you know how much you've gained or given up. Now you can adjust the price.

This approach doesn't guarantee you'll get acceptance on every point, but you're strategizing on getting information, giving information, getting information, giving information—to the end goal of achieving your most important point. Remember, a negotiation is meant to result in a win-win for all involved.

While you are moving down the list and tackling each issue, you can modify the order of agenda items if the negotiation dictates that you do so. For example, you may want to say, "John, in regard to the next two items, let's put them to the side for now and get back to them later."

An agenda also helps memorialize the event, especially if you write lots of notes on the agenda sheet itself. Doing this makes it harder for the other party to dispute that you discussed a particular issue. Having an agenda also makes it easier for you to write your follow-up correspondence after the negotiation session.

SUMMARY POINTS FOR CHAPTER 13: BUYERS—TAKING THE DRIVER'S SEAT

- To protect themselves from vulture or opportunity buyers, sellers need to be cautious and not reveal that they're experiencing financial hemorrhaging.
- When the values start to trend downward and you need or want to sell, prepare for your negotiation by getting your property appraised, converting an adjustable rate mortgage to a fixed rate mortgage, being prepared to provide financing to the buyer of your property, including your bottom-line price and last closing date in your broker's contract, and building a matrix of comparables.
- Look beyond the ordinary in all your negotiations as you think outside the box.
- Carefully choose the best location for your negotiation session depending on the objectives you've set for that session.
- By writing an agenda and distributing it at the negotiation meeting, you control what subjects will be discussed and in what order. Make a habit of doing so.

14

A WORD ABOUT ETHICS

Only morality in our actions can give beauty and dignity to our lives.

Albert Einstein

I believe it's paramount that you conduct your real estate negotiations ethically. In business, especially in real estate, your reputation is everything. Usually the real estate community in a town or even in a city is rather small. If you develop a reputation for being a straight shooter—someone who negotiates fairly—it will only benefit you in your future negotiations.

You want people to respect you and say this about you: "He may drive a hard bargain, but he's a reputable negotiator." If you prove this to be true time and again, people will want to bring reputable real estate deals to you.

On the other hand, if you behave unethically, it will cost you in the long run. Once others mark you as disreputable and unethical, your reputation in the real estate circles will precede you, keeping you from getting good deals and working with honest people.

THE VALUE OF ETHICAL NEGOTIATIONS

A good friend of mine, Christian Deutsch, once told me a story about his first job as a purchasing agent. His story illustrates how it's easy to be challenged to make the right ethical decision.

Chris was a 27-year-old, newly hired purchasing agent for a major manufacturing company in Pittsburgh, Pennsylvania. The company needed to purchase a lot of bronze ingot, often purchasing $20 million to $30 million worth every year. The current purchasing agent was retiring and Chris was reaching the tail end of his six-month training program, working every day next to the company's chief purchasing agent, Frank.

Chris soon learned that this agent always purchased the ingot from the same three suppliers every year. Even more interesting, the suppliers had always charged list price and the company had always paid it. Little negotiating ever took place.

Chris had learned in college that supply and demand determines price. He believed that because the company was purchasing such a large volume of ingot, it should be able to negotiate a discounted price. So he discussed this with Frank and asked permission to be able to collect bids from the three suppliers. Feeling apprehensive, Frank told Chris that's the way it was always done. Bidding it out would be a waste of time because the prices would only come back at the list price. However, Frank gave Chris the go-ahead to do what he thought was best.

A few days later, Chris's wife Sandy received a gift in the mail from one of the ingot suppliers. He emphatically told his wife not to keep it. Then he brought the gift in to work, placed it on Frank's desk, and demanded to know what he wanted to do with it.

Surprised, Frank asked Chris why he wanted to return the gift. "You're on the gift list now!" he exclaimed, as if it was a huge privilege. Chris couldn't believe that an actual gift list existed. This list specified the various executives in the organization who were allowed to accept gifts from suppliers. He told Frank he thought this practice was wrong and insisted on the company negotiating the price through a sealed bid process.

Chris reviewed the gift list and noticed a shipping clerk's name was on the list. He thought this was highly unusual because the shipping clerk was a low-ranked employee in the company. When he went down to the shipping area to see who the clerk was, he found the clerk cleaning the bronze ingot with a hose. Because the ingot was going to be melted down at the plant, doing this wasteful activity was absolutely ludicrous.

Then Chris watched as the truck filled with just-washed ingot moved to the scale to be weighed. The company was actually *over paying* for the ingot because of the addition of its own water! He now understood why the shipping clerk was on the gift list.

So Chris put his negotiation plan into action. He sent out a Request for Proposal (RFP) to all three suppliers and announced that the low bidder would get the majority of the business. The three suppliers were from New Jersey, Chicago, and western Pennsylvania. One week later, all three bids arrived at the same time and all were postmarked from Chicago. More than that, all of the bids came in with the same list price.

Chris was furious. He placed the three bids face down on Frank's desk, asking him to pick one. Frank chose randomly and picked the western Pennsylvania supplier. Chris looked at it and declared, "This is the supplier we will give all the business to."

Intuitively, Chris knew that the three suppliers didn't trust each other; otherwise they would have sent the bids in from their respective cities. The representative for the western Pennsylvania supplier was delighted that he received the whole order—except that it did put him in a precarious situation with the other two suppliers. That day, the other two suppliers called Chris and wanted to meet with him privately. One of the suppliers invited Chris for lunch. Although he was only making $26,000 a year at the time, Chris told the supplier that he'd pay for his own lunch. On the way to the restaurant, the supplier pulled into a Cadillac dealership and offered Chris a brand-new car valued at $8,000. Chris frankly told the supplier that he would ignore the offer, saying, "My company and I are only looking for quality and a good price."

Two weeks later, Chris sent another RFP out to the three suppliers and asked them to bid more wisely. The bids came in at least 28 percent lower than the list price. He awarded the contract to the true lowest bidder. The savings to the company, if it were computed in today's dollars, was well over $30 million in one year.

The top executives were elated because they would all receive bonuses for realizing such a substantial savings. The CEO thanked Chris wholeheartedly and said that if there was anything he could do, just ask. Taking quick advantage of the opportunity, Chris took out from his breast pocket a brochure on an MBA Executive program he wanted to attend but couldn't because the $10,000 tuition was too expensive. The CEO smiled, shook Chris's hand, and told him, "Consider it done."

In negotiating or in bidding, people are often tempted to take the easy way out or look the other way. In reality, if you do what is right and keep a steady moral compass pointed in the direction of high ethical behavior, you, too, will be rewarded as Chris was.

SUMMARY POINTS FOR CHAPTER 14: A WORD ABOUT ETHICS

- If you've proven to be an ethical person time and time again, people will want to bring reputable real estate deals to you.
- In negotiating or in bidding, people are often tempted to take the easy way out or look the other way, but you'll be rewarded if you do what is right and keep a steady moral compass pointed in the direction of high ethical behavior.

15

ROLE-PLAYING AS NEGOTIATORS

Think three times before taking the first step.

Chinese proverb

All great professionals practice their craft by rehearsing and role-playing. Negotiators sharpen their skills by experiencing the trials and tribulations of actual negotiations. However, well-thought-out role-playing with a genuine goal of re-creating that negotiation can clearly help the person who wants to hone his or her skills.

The following pages are full of tools to use in role-playing. For effective learning, I ask you to commit to using the honor system and not read the role-playing pages in Appendix G that correspond with this exercise. Instead, read the description for your character in each of the three situations described. You'll find your opponent's profile in the role-playing exercises in Appendix G.

I recommend you divide your role-playing into three segments:

1. The first segment should be five minutes long. At the sound of the timer, immediately stop the negotiation and take a two-minute break to gather your thoughts, review any notes you've made, and plan your next moves.
2. The second segment should be four minutes long, stopped by the sound of the timer, and followed by a two-minute break.

3. The third and final segment should be only three minutes long, and both negotiators should understand that the deal must be closed during this round.

If you have access to a video camera, you may find it beneficial to film the role-playing. Think of yourself as if you were a professional athlete; continually review your own performance and practice your skills to perfection.

The two main guidelines to keep in mind when role-playing are as follows:

1. You must follow the script and the profile as best as you can.
2. You must come to some agreement.

SCENARIO ONE—THE MANAGER AND THE EMPLOYEE

This role-playing warm-up exercise helps you feel comfortable pretending to be involved in a negotiation. This negotiation is typical—so typical, in fact, that a similar scenario is probably happening somewhere in the world at this moment.

In this situation, an employee has asked to meet with his manager to request a raise.

Go to Script Number One and become familiar with the particular situation that the employee faces. Hand this book to a colleague and ask him or her to turn to Appendix G and read the profile and script for the manager.

Before you begin the role-play, make sure that you and your colleague understand the rules and set a time limit for the duration of the role-play.

Script Number One—The Employee

You are a loyal employee seeking a raise.

Your situation is as follows:

- You have worked in the company for five years.
- Your performance is slightly above average.
- The job market is bad and you need this job.
- You would like a raise of at least 4 percent and an additional week of vacation.
- The manager you're speaking with has the authority to reduce the workforce, if necessary.

(See Appendix G for manager's script.)

Did You Notice?

During the role-play, did you notice that once you got into the numbers, the discussion heated up? It's amazing how uncomfortable people get, even in mock situations, when the subject of money is discussed. Imagine the extra pressure present in a real-life situation and you can see the importance of practicing through role-plays!

SCENARIO TWO—THE BUYER AND THE SELLER

This role-playing exercise relates directly to real estate. Ask your colleague to read the profile and script for the buyer (again see Appendix G). The rules of the game are the same as for Scenario One. Be sure to stick to the profile and aim to reach an agreement within the allotted time.

When I conduct these exercises in the classroom, I act as a mediator. In this role, I observe the two parties carefully, making notes about the positive aspects of their negotiating skills as well as their shortcomings. I stop them every three to five minutes to discuss what they're doing right and what they're doing wrong. In a similar way, you may want to ask a third party to observe the role-play and provide unbiased constructive criticism.

Script Number Two—The Seller

You own a property worth approximately $500,000.

Your situation is as follows:

- You must sell the property because you just landed a big job in California.
- You're asking $520,000 for it.
- You don't want the buyer to know you have a deadline.
- The property needs renovation but you don't have time to fix it up.
- Your bottom-line price is $425,000.
- You'd be willing to hold the mortgage.

(See Appendix G for buyer's script.)

Did You Notice?

During the role-play, did you notice that it's important to watch for verbal and nonverbal cues? For example, in one of my classes, the buyer asked the seller why he was selling. He hadn't considered how to cover his urgent need to sell before he moved out of state, so he literally took a step back before answering this way: "My family is growing and we need more room, so we're moving into a bigger house." If the buyer paid attention to his nonverbal cue, she would have wondered what he was covering up. She might have uncovered his real motivation for selling, thereby gaining an advantage.

What is the lesson here? As a buyer, always ask "Why are you selling?" and "Would you lower the price?"

Remember, the way people answer questions will give you clues about whether they are firm or have wiggle room. If your opponent is bluffing or acting tough, ignore the pretense. Indicate you heard him, but will continue in your negotiation. And don't be afraid to shoot out a lowball offer. It gives you a chance to study the seller's reaction. You'll gather a lot of information and just might gain extra dollars.

One strategy a seller can use is to keep stating the word "flexible" in response to the buyer's questions. It signals to the buyer that you're open to suggestions, but you're not giving away too much information.

Another strategy is to draw the buyer in by agreeing with the statements in theory, then clarifying the details. For example, to overcome an objection on repairs, you might say, "Yes, it needs some work, but it's minor, not major. I've hired a contractor and he's provided a report spelling out the needed repairs." The initial agreement disarms your opponent, putting that person at ease. You then show your strength with your knowledge and preparation.

Yet another strategy for a seller to use is a common practice in negotiating: deferring to higher authority by saying, "I'll have to talk to my partner first" or "I'm not sure my spouse will go for that." Say this after your opponent has already shown his or her hand. If you're the buyer on the other side of that pitch, how do you get around it? You always make sure the decision maker is present from the beginning, or don't negotiate. Yes, you can wait.

For both sides, asking "What is your best offer?" and "What's the best you can do?" and "What's your bottom line?" are all good questions when used at the right moment in the negotiation.

SCENARIO THREE—THE LANDLORD AND THE TENANT

This real-world scenario also involves a real estate investor. Again, ask your role-playing colleague to read the script for the tenant from Appendix G. Get your alarm or stopwatch ready, and . . . go!

Script Number Three—The Landlord

You are the landlord of a small, mixed-use building (a building with both commercial and residential tenants).

Your situation is as follows:

- You're trying to lease the ground floor to a commercial tenant.
- The space has been empty for quite some time and needs repairs, but you don't have a great deal of extra cash to finance the repairs.
- You're asking $50 per square foot per year for the rent. You'd like to achieve $48 per square foot per year. Your bottom line is $43 per square foot per year.
- You want the tenant to pay for the electricity.
- Because rents are going down, you want to lock in a long-term lease (ten years).

- You need to find a good tenant quickly.
- You'll only give two months of free rent because you've already lost a great deal of potential rent.
- If you lose this potential tenant, it may be quite a while before you find another.

(See Appendix G for tenant's script.)

BUILD YOUR EXPERIENCE

While role-playing is inherently more relaxed than the real deal—after all, nothing of consequence is at stake—it's still difficult to re-create the real-life negotiation with all of the excitement, stress, and spontaneity that may be present in a real estate negotiation. To make the role-playing more realistic, I emphasize that you must impose time limits. In addition, you may want to create your own scenarios using the above scenarios as guidelines.

Remember, when you're negotiating with another person, the exchange between you is never equal. Often, one person will have a lot more experience in negotiating than the other, so that person will know how to "push" the deal. Role-playing helps you build the experience you want to bring to the table.

I suggest you practice with different people and make a point to experience different personalities and emotional makeups. Learn how to "push" the deal in the direction you want it to go so it's a win-win experience that ensures you achieve your most critical elements.

The negotiation process can be fraught with intensity and confusion as each party tries to make sense of the factors and motivations involved and then come to a mutually acceptable agreement. I don't recommend trying to "wing it" if your mind is in a state of intensity and confusion. Instead, develop a plan and practice it through role-playing before sitting down at the negotiation table.

16

NEGOTIATING AROUND THE WORLD—CULTURAL NUANCES

The fundamentals of negotiating are similar throughout the world; however, make a point of becoming aware of cultural nuances when negotiating with people from different countries. If you are fascinated with the concepts of negotiating with various peoples, I encourage you to research the topic in more detail. When you do, you'll certainly be rewarded.

KNOW YOUR NATIVE STYLE

Before you negotiate with someone from another country or culture, observe the way people naturally negotiate in your native country or culture. My advice is to not try to mimic the other country's negotiating style. Indeed, this is impossible. There are too many nuances, traditions, and attitudes that would take years to understand and implement properly. I do suggest that you take into account these important factors:

- Innovation
- Impatience

- Confidence versus arrogance
- Lone gunslinger versus group dynamics
- Negotiating before building trust

Let's discuss each of these in detail.

Innovation

As Americans, I think it's helpful to preserve our business philosophy of independent thinking and openness, and to nurture our drive to innovate and "think outside the box."

I also think it's important to identify those areas of the typical American negotiating style that could cause you embarrassment, unnecessary friction, or a misunderstanding.

Impatience

Americans would benefit from being acutely aware of their seemingly innate impatience as it is viewed by people from other cultures around the globe. That means an overriding characteristic required of Americans in negotiating with any foreigner is patience. Generally, Americans (especially urbanites) operate in a fast-paced manner compared with people around the world. The advantage to slowing down is that slower-paced negotiations can prevent you from conceding too much too fast, and they also can reduce misunderstandings.

Confidence versus Arrogance

Many American businesspeople exude an overly confident attitude that is apparent to foreign businesspeople. This ethnocentric behavior can start the negotiations off on the wrong foot. You're advised to show humility along the way. When you do, you'll still be able to use all of your business intelligence, strategic abilities, and negotiating prowess. I suggest that you carry out your negotiations with a foreigner in a less self-centered way than you might in the United States.

Lone Gunslinger versus Group Dynamics

Many other cultures use a group approach to negotiating rather than the American style found in a Western movie's lone gunslinger role. In most cultures, negotiation strategies and decisions are made by a group. However, in the United States, it's common for one person to be charged with devising the strategy and carrying it out.

It's wise for an American negotiator to respect the concept of group process negotiation, which is the root reason why negotiations with foreigners take longer than might be expected.

Negotiating before Building Trust

While trust building before a negotiation session is not completely absent in America, it's not a required prerequisite, either. However, in most foreign cultures, it's imperative that a relationship be formed and a bond of trust be established before any meaningful negotiation can take place. Many Americans skip this step or don't spend enough time developing a meaningful business relationship. Trying to cut a fast deal or to continually speed up negotiations will only be detrimental to the negotiations in the long run.

KNOW YOUR OPPONENT'S STYLE

Understanding the constitution, government style, and day-to-day life of people in another country often helps when negotiating a transaction in that country. Here's a comparison.

British and French Negotiators

The British use a subtle, less direct approach in negotiations—more of a soft-selling style—than Americans. British negotiators use more tact and decorum during the negotiation. They're more reserved and display less emotion than Americans. The British conduct long, drawn-out debates and prefer a rational approach to their negotiations. They handle discussions in a highly proper manner.

Similar to how they live their everyday lives, French people enjoy a lively debate, which translates into their negotiation style. Their approach may appear argumentative, but it is their way of analyzing every facet of each negotiation point. To the French businessperson, the negotiation will be a combination of a formal event and an intellectual debate.

Chinese Negotiators

I have been involved in numerous transactions with Chinese negotiators in both mainland China and Taiwan, traveling to rural areas as well as major cities. What I've learned from these negotiations can be summarized as follows:

- Chinese negotiators have plenty of room to maneuver with regard to price because they tend to over inflate their required goal. For example, if a Chinese negotiator is willing to spend up to $1 million for a piece of property, he might start his offer at $500,000.
- A Chinese negotiator ranks opponents according to their Guanxi, which means connections. It is also important that a trusted friend or colleague introduce one businessperson to another. This go-between person plays an important role in the negotiations.
- Chinese people admire stick-to-it-iveness and respect those who have a long history of negotiating or managing a business.

Most important, I have found that my Chinese counterparts focus on "the way," or to what they refer to as the "Tao," which means sometimes they focus more on the *process* of getting to the goal rather than on the goal *itself*.

To understand the Chinese negotiator better, I recommend doing research on the Mandarin language and beliefs. The Mandarin language is fascinating. I'm always impressed by my two Chinese friends, Nelson Li and Kevin Hu, both born in mainland China. They had to memorize thousands upon thousands of pictograms to learn their language. And to excel in real estate, they had to learn English and the specific business jargon related to this industry.

Chinese pictograms have to be read as a whole to understand the meaning of the sentence. This is quite different than English in which one word gets read at a time. For this reason, a Chinese negotiator tends to look at the whole picture all at once, while an American negotiator looks at a negotiation in a sequence. For a Chinese negotiator, the big picture comes first and the details become secondary.

Understanding the Chinese negotiator also requires a fundamental understanding of Confucianism and Taoism. Confucianism is a philosophical system based on the teachings of Confucius (Kong Fuzi, c. 551–479 BCE). This philosophy defines the Tao ("the way") as "virtuous conduct stemming from universal criteria and ideals governing existence." Taoism is a system of philosophy and religion based on the teachings of Lao-tzu (sixth century BCE). It advocates preserving and restoring the Tao in the body and the cosmos, defining it as the basic, eternal principle of the universe that transcends reality. It's the source of being, non-being, and change.

Because of these cultural differences, Chinese negotiators find it difficult to easily trust an American negotiator. That trust must truly be earned.

Japanese Negotiators

The business style of the Japanese is quite formal and stems from the beginnings of their government and society. In 648 AD, Prince Shotoku created the constitution of 17 Articles. The key components of this constitution, which still typify the mind and spirit of many modern Japanese, are the following:

- Formal politeness should be the leading principle in your interaction with other people.
- Judge people fairly.
- Loyalty, trust, and sincerity are the foundations of virtue.

THE CONCEPT OF WHOLENESS IN JAPAN

In the early 1990s, I lived in Tokyo, Japan, which gave me a wonderful opportunity to travel the country and meet executives and managers of companies. During that time, I conducted 66 presentations to various top Japanese companies and negotiated real estate transactions with many of them. I learned to deal with many compelling differences in the Japanese style of negotiating versus the American style.

For example, Japanese negotiators start from the whole first. This means that when they negotiate, they see the entirety of the negotiation beforehand. They try to grasp the whole contract before beginning to negotiate. This approach requires an enormous amount of data collection and research, which is the prime reason why, in most cases, Japanese negotiations may take longer than the impatient American negotiator is used to. The Japanese refer to this concept as "Nemawashi," which can be translated into the phrase "root binding" or "laying the groundwork."

Pricing Not the Most Important Element

Pricing may not be a major factor in the strategy of Japanese negotiators. They usually stick to the asking price or very close to it. Instead, they prefer to change certain elements of the negotiation, for example, adding more customer service or removing some of the benefit. In fact, changing the price during a negotiation can be interpreted as mistrust. Benefits and timing are clearly important to the Japanese negotiator.

Asking Price versus Selling Price

In the United States, the swing between the asking price and selling price ranges from 10 to 20 percent. This means that if you want to sell a property for $1 million, you would advertise it for $1.25 million.

In Latin American and Chinese countries, the swing is usually greater—20 to 50 percent in negotiations. Why the difference? Because that's the way things run culturally; haggling is considered fun.

But in Japan, the swing ranges from 0 to 10 percent. The price is the price. Japanese people will add or subtract quality, service, or some other component, but not price. They perceive that any move off the stated price is deception. Asking for a change breeds mistrust, so they prefer to agree on the price and then add elements to it or subtract elements from it.

Who **P**ays for the **E**lectricity? **A** **C**ase **S**tudy in **J**apanese **N**egotiation

I recall one major negotiation I had with a Japanese firm that drove home the distinct differences between our styles of negotiation.

The executive I reported to told me that a breakdown had occurred in our company's relationship and negotiations with a major tenant at our office park. He explained that the Japanese company owed us $1.2 million, was behind in the payment, and refused to pay. Because I was studying the Japanese language and becoming familiar with their negotiation style, I was asked to arrange for the negotiation session. My assignment was to get them to pay the $1.2 million owed for the electricity costs.

I first set out to contact the person who was of equal rank to me at the Japanese company. The Japanese have a great respect for hierarchy in both government and in business, therefore it would have been imprudent for me to contact someone at a higher or lower level. So I called Mr. Nagakawa, who had the same title I did, and politely requested that we schedule a meeting to discuss the situation. I invited him to a neutral meeting place so he would not feel uncomfortable at our office, and so I would not show weakness by going to his office.

The Japanese do not have a litigious society. If I had brought a number of contracts and agreements to stick under his nose while trying to prove my righteousness, it would have been a disaster. I brought only myself. I had no paperwork, no briefcase. I arrived early and waited in the conference room for Mr. Nagakawa. When the phone rang in the conference room, I spoke to the receptionist, who explained that seven people in the lobby were waiting for me. I kindly (and wrongly) informed the receptionist that she was mistaken, that I was only waiting for Mr. Nakagawa. But to my surprise, Mr. Nakagawa had brought six of his colleagues with him. I exchanged pleasantries and business cards with my guests. I bowed to the appropriate depth. To those I'd never met, I politely said, "Haji-may-ma-shta," which means, "It is a pleasure to make your acquaintance."

I asked Mr. Nakagawa to sit at the round conference table, indicating his seat was the one allowing him to face the entrance door to the conference room. In Japanese society, the most revered seat in a room is the one farthest from the door and still facing it. This seat provides a clear view of the exit, and is the most protected seat because no one can attack the person in this seat from behind or from either side. In

Asian culture, granting the view of the door signifies reverence and respect. Who's more powerful—the one giving the reverence or the one receiving it? It's as if the warden were giving the prisoner freedom.

After Mr. Nakagawa took his seat, I directed his colleagues to their seats—three to his left and three to his right. I asked if he would be so kind as to make clear the situation to me. He carefully explained that my office park representatives built a large electrical network for his company's use, that this was part of the lease negotiation. He explained that the lease included a section stating that the office park would provide his company with the electrical network. He also stated that his company was surprised to receive a bill for $1.2 million. He further elaborated that the English dictionary defines the phrase "to provide" as "to give." In other words, he believed that the office park was supposed to give his company the electrical network at no cost to his company.

I did not reply immediately. I looked at Mr. Nakagawa and only at Mr. Nakagawa. Slowly and methodically, I explained that it was true. The lease document does say that the office park is required to give his company the electrical network. I explained this was a convenience for his company and the security consideration for our company. It was very important for the good of the entire office park that our men, who were most familiar with the overall electrical infrastructure of the office park, design and install the electrical network. As in all the documents that we give our tenants, I said there is also a reimbursement section. In the reimbursement part of the lease, it's explained that these types of conveniences installed for the tenant must be reimbursed in a timely manner. I further explained that another tenant, Merrill Lynch, had the same exact requirement in its lease document.

I said nothing more.

Much time elapsed as Mr. Nakagawa and I looked at each other. After what seemed an eternity, Mr. Nakagawa finally said, "Sumi-ma-sen," which means "excuse me" in Japanese. He then conferred quietly with his colleagues on his left for a few minutes, and then conferred with his colleagues on his right. He looked back at me and confidently stated, "I understand; we will pay you." I was surprised, but did not let my Japanese guests know that I was pleased with their response.

Later, I related the event to a Japanese executive. He explained that they had used a traditional style of Japanese team negotiations and group consensus in decision making. He also stated that the seven of them were all watching me carefully to see if I gave any verbal or nonverbal cues that I was lying or misleading them. He said I must have appeared comfortable with seven men against one. Because our respective companies had a good relationship prior to this situation, I was telling the truth, and my explanation made a great deal of sense to them, so they agreed to pay us. One week later, the entire $1.2 million was wire-transferred from Tokyo to our company.

The lesson here, especially in a high-stakes negotiation, is to become familiar with the people you are negotiating with. Understand their motivation, their country's general style of negotiating, their goals, and their abilities. *Semper Paratus*—Always Prepared.

UNDERSTANDING THE OTHER PARTY'S BELIEF SYSTEM

During one of the many international negotiations I participated in at the World Trade Center, I learned why it's important to understand the other party's belief system and intentions before engaging in a negotiation. Here's what happened.

In early 1991, I was in charge of International Leasing for the World Trade Center in New York. The late 1980s was the time of "perestroika" (defined as restructuring or reconstruction) in Russia—Mikhail Gorbachev's program of economic, political, and social restructuring. At that time, our goal at the World Trade Center was to create a "House of International Commerce." In my role, I would assist companies that were based in emerging markets (like Russia, for example) in building their U.S. business outposts.

The new Russian government wanted to establish a Russian Trade Center inside the World Trade Center complex. It would be a place for American businesspeople to learn about buying and selling products and resources from Russia and to meet with Russian business executives. The prime minister of Russia at the time was Ivan Stepanovich Silayev, who served in this position from June 1990 to September 1991. After being replaced as prime minister by Boris Yeltsin, he served as the representative of Russia in the European Community between 1991 and 1994.

Sensitivity between the United States and Russia was extremely high at this time. We arranged a clandestine meeting among Silayev and his negotiation team, our World Trade Center executives, and the U.S. government's negotiation team. We had to work closely with the Secret Service to arrange the meeting inside the World Trade Center on a weekend afternoon. (Today, I have a wonderful, rare memento from the meeting. I asked the Russian prime minister to sign the cover of an American magazine called *Business in the USSR*. Little did I know that he would hold the position of prime minister of Russia for such a short time. It is highly unlikely that he gave his autograph to any other American while he was in power.)

Our negotiations focused on the Russian government's desire to lease a large block of space at the World Trade Center for a lengthy term.

During the negotiations, we came to an impasse. To appease the other side, we offered the Russian team the ability to sublease its space to another company. We explained that if the company who was subleasing the space was willing to pay the Russians more rent than they paid, the Russians could keep the profit. Once the translator explained our kind gesture, the gentlemen on the Russian side became agitated and insulted. They thought we were offering them something illegal or asking them to do something corrupt. From their point of view, they assumed we were suggesting that if they failed in their main business, they could turn around and still make a profit on the misfortune.

These gentlemen had never been exposed to the concept of subleasing. And we'd taken it for granted that they understood it! Consequently, it took hours for us to explain what was customary in the United States and how subleasing worked.

That day, I learned how important it is to keep the other person's point of view in mind at all times. It's also important to continually explain your reasoning before submitting your offers or suggesting changes to an offer.

SUMMARY POINTS FOR CHAPTER 16: NEGOTIATING AROUND THE WORLD— CULTURAL NUANCES

- Before negotiating with someone from another country or culture, first observe the way people naturally negotiate in your native country or culture.
- Don't try to mimic the other country's negotiating style. Instead, take into account the following factors: innovation, impatience, confidence versus arrogance, lone gunslinger versus group dynamics, and negotiating before building trust.
- Understanding the constitution, government style, and day-to-day life of people in another country often helps when negotiating a transaction in that country.
- Learn the nuances of business in other countries. Understand their motivation, their country's general style of negotiating, their goals, and their abilities. Keep the other person's point of view in mind at all times, and explain your reasoning before submitting offers or suggesting changes to an offer.

A

CHOICES FOR ORGANIZATIONAL STRUCTURE

The following information came from Small Business Success, a workshop series sponsored by the Ohio Women's Business Resource Network. Courtesy of the U.S. Small Business Administration (http://www.sba.gov/starting_business/legal/forms.html).

SOLE PROPRIETORSHIPS

The vast majority of small businesses start out as sole proprietorships. These firms are owned by one person, usually the individual who has day-to-day responsibility for running the business. Sole proprietors own all the assets of the business and the profits generated by it. They also assume complete responsibility for any of its liabilities or debts. In the eyes of the law and the public, you are one and the same with the business.

Advantages of a Sole Proprietorship

- It's the easiest and least expensive form of ownership to organize.
- Sole proprietors are in complete control, and within the parameters of the law, may make decisions as they see fit.

- Sole proprietors receive all income generated by the business to keep or reinvest.
- Profits from the business flow through directly to the owner's personal tax return.
- The business is easy to dissolve, if desired.

Disadvantages of a Sole Proprietorship

- Sole proprietors have unlimited liability and are legally responsible for all debts against the business. Their business and personal assets are at risk.
- They may be at a disadvantage in raising funds and are often limited to using funds from personal savings or consumer loans.
- They may have a hard time attracting high-caliber employees, or those that are motivated by the opportunity to own a part of the business.
- Some employee benefits, such as owner's medical insurance premiums, are not directly deductible from business income (only partially deductible as an adjustment to income).

Federal Tax Forms for Sole Proprietorships

(partial list; some may not apply)

- Form 1040: Individual Income Tax Return
- Schedule C: Profit or Loss from Business (or Schedule C-EZ)
- Schedule SE: Self-Employment Tax
- Form 1040-ES: Estimated Tax for Individuals
- Form 4562: Depreciation and Amortization
- Form 8829: Expenses for Business Use of Your Home
- Employment Tax Forms

PARTNERSHIPS

In a partnership, two or more people share ownership of a single business. Like proprietorships, the law does not distinguish between the business and its owners. The partners should have a legal agreement that sets forth how decisions will be made, profits will be shared, disputes will be resolved, how future partners will be admitted to the partnership, how partners can be bought out, or what steps will be taken to dissolve the partnership when needed.

Yes, it's hard to think about a "break up" when the business is just getting started, but many partnerships split up at crisis times and unless there is a defined process, there will be even greater problems. They also must decide up front how much time and capital each will contribute, etc.

Advantages of a Partnership

- Partnerships are relatively easy to establish; however, time should be invested in developing the partnership agreement.
- With more than one owner, the ability to raise funds may be increased.
- The profits from the business flow directly through to the partners' personal tax returns.
- Prospective employees may be attracted to the business if given the incentive to become a partner.
- The business usually will benefit from partners who have complementary skills.

Disadvantages of a Partnership

- Partners are jointly and individually liable for the actions of the other partners.
- Profits must be shared with others.
- Since decisions are shared, disagreements can occur.
- Some employee benefits are not deductible from business income on tax returns.
- The partnership may have a limited life; it may end upon the withdrawal or death of a partner.

Types of Partnerships

1. *General partnership.* Partners divide responsibility for management and liability, as well as the shares of profit or loss according to their internal agreement. Equal shares are assumed unless there is a written agreement that states differently.

2. *Limited partnership and partnership with limited liability.* "Limited" means that most of the partners have limited liability (to the extent of their investment), as well as limited input regarding management decisions, which generally encourages investors for short-term projects, or for investing in capital assets. This form of ownership is not often used for operating retail or service businesses. Forming a limited partnership is more complex and formal than that of a general partnership.

3. *Joint venture.* Acts like a general partnership, but is clearly for a limited period of time or a single project. If the partners in a joint venture repeat the activity, they will be recognized as an ongoing partnership and will have to file as such, and distribute accumulated partnership assets upon dissolution of the entity.

Federal Tax Forms for Partnerships

(partial list; some may not apply)

- Form 1065: Partnership Return of Income
- Form 1065 K-1: Partner's Share of Income, Credit, Deductions
- Form 4562: Depreciation
- Form 1040: Individual Income Tax Return
- Schedule E: Supplemental Income and Loss
- Schedule SE: Self-Employment Tax
- Form 1040-ES: Estimated Tax for Individuals
- Employment Tax Forms

CORPORATIONS

A corporation, chartered by the state in which it is headquartered, is considered by law to be a unique entity, separate and apart from those who own it. A corporation can be taxed; it can be sued; it can enter into contractual agreements. The owners of a corporation are its shareholders. The shareholders elect a board of directors to oversee the major policies and decisions. The corporation has a life of its own and does not dissolve when ownership changes.

Advantages of a Corporation

- Shareholders have limited liability for the corporation's debts or judgments against the corporations.
- Generally, shareholders can only be held accountable for their investment in stock of the company. (Note, however, that officers can be held personally liable for their actions, such as the failure to withhold and pay employment taxes.)
- Corporations can raise additional funds through the sale of stock.
- A corporation may deduct the cost of benefits it provides to officers and employees.
- It can elect S corporation status if certain requirements are met. This election enables a company to be taxed similar to a partnership.

Disadvantages of a Corporation

- The process of incorporation requires more time and money than other forms of organization.
- Corporations are monitored by federal, state, and some local agencies, and as a result may have more paperwork to comply with regulations.
- Incorporating may result in higher overall taxes. Dividends paid to shareholders are not deductible from business income, thus this income can be taxed twice.

Federal Tax Forms for Regular or "C" Corporations

(partial list; some may not apply)

- Form 1120 or 1120-A: Corporation Income Tax Return
- Form 1120-W: Estimated Tax for Corporation

- Form 8109-B: Deposit Coupon
- Form 4625: Depreciation
- Employment Tax Forms

Other forms as needed for capital gains, sale of assets, alternative minimum tax, etc.

SUBCHAPTER S CORPORATIONS

A tax election only; this election enables the shareholder to treat the earnings and profits as distributions, and have them pass through directly to their personal tax return. The catch here is that the shareholder, if working for the company, and if there is a profit, must pay herself wages, and it must meet standards of "reasonable compensation." This can vary by geographical region as well as occupation, but the basic rule is to pay yourself what you would have to pay someone to do your job, as long as there is enough profit. If you do not do this, the IRS can reclassify all of the earnings and profit as wages, and you will be liable for all of the payroll taxes on the total amount.

Federal Tax Forms for Subchapter S Corporations

(partial list; some may not apply)

- Form 1120S: Income Tax Return for S Corporation
- 1120S K-1: Shareholder's Share of Income, Credit, Deductions
- Form 4625: Depreciation
- Employment Tax Forms
- Form 1040: Individual Income Tax Return
- Schedule E: Supplemental Income and Loss
- Schedule SE: Self-Employment Tax
- Form 1040-ES: Estimated Tax for Individuals

Other forms as needed for capital gains, sale of assets, alternative minimum tax, etc.

LIMITED LIABILITY COMPANY (LLC)

The LLC is a relatively new type of hybrid business structure that is now permissible in most states. It is designed to provide the limited liability features of a corporation and the tax efficiencies and operational flexibility of a partnership. Formation is more complex and formal than that of a general partnership. The owners are members, and the duration of the LLC is usually determined when the organization papers are filed. The time limit can be continued if desired by a vote of the members at the time of expiration. LLCs must not have more than two of the four characteristics that define corporations: limited liability to the extent of assets; continuity of life; centralization of management; and free transferability of ownership interests.

Federal Tax Forms for LLCs

Taxed as partnership in most cases; corporation forms must be used if there are more than two of the four corporate characteristics, as described above.

In summary, deciding the form of ownership that best suits your business venture should be given careful consideration. Use your key advisors to assist you in the process.

B

SAMPLE
BROKERAGE AGREEMENTS

TYPICAL REAL ESTATE
BROKERAGE AGREEMENT

Date: _____

Re: _____(address of property)

Dear Mr. _____,

You have employed (name of brokerage company) as a real estate broker with an "Exclusive Right to Sell" Agreement for the sale of the above captioned property. An "Exclusive Right to Sell" means that if you, the owner, find a buyer, or another broker finds a buyer, the agreed commission will be due to the exclusive broker.

The terms of this agreement are as follows:

1. This agreement shall be effective as of _____, 200__. It shall continue in full force and effect until _____, 200__, except that

this agreement may be terminated after said six-month period by either party on thirty (30) days' prior notice in writing to the other; but upon and after the effective date of such termination, client shall continue to recognize <u>(name of brokerage company)</u> as its exclusive agent in any negotiations then pending or begun prior thereto, whether by <u>(name of brokerage company)</u>, client, or anyone else.

2. If the property is sold pursuant to this agreement, <u>(name of brokerage company)</u>'s commission to be paid by you will be six percent (6%) of the total sale price. This commission will be payable at the closing.

3. It is further understood by us that if the closing is not consummated for any cause or reason whatsoever after the contract of sale has been executed, except due to the willful default of the Seller, the commission set forth above is not due and payable, and we shall not have any claim whatsoever against you for a commission, or other compensation, in connection with this transaction.

4. We will offer the property through our own organization and direct and oversee its sale. We will report to you so that you are informed of all pertinent developments.

5. As part of our marketing campaign we will advertise the property at our own expense.

6. You hereby authorize us to solicit the cooperation of other licensed real estate brokers who will act as agents for the prospective purchasers, and to work with them on a cooperating basis. In the event another licensed real state broker is involved in the transaction, we will split the commission with such broker and in no event will negotiate the commission paid by you to exceed six percent (6%) of the sale price.

7. We will arrange whatever appointments may be necessary to show the property to prospective purchasers at times convenient to you.

8. We will handle all negotiations and submit to you any offers we receive.

9. You agree to refer all inquiries concerning the sale of the property to us.

10. Within ten (10) days after the expiration of the listing term we shall deliver to you a list of no more than fifteen (15) names of persons who inspected the premises during the listing term. If within six (6) months after the expiration of the listing term a contract is signed to sell the premises to a person on said list, we shall be entitled to the commission provided for in this agreement.

11. This agreement shall bind and benefit the personal representatives, successors, or assigns of the parties. This agreement may not be changed, rescinded, or modified except in writing, signed by both parties.

12. In the event that you become legally entitled to retain any deposit paid to you pursuant to a signed contract of sale, by a person introduced during the term of this agreement, you agree to pay six percent (6%) of that amount to (name of brokerage company). This payment shall be nonrefundable, provided, however, that it shall be credited toward the partial satisfaction of any commission that may subsequently become due. The payment shall not become due, however, unless and until you, as Seller, receive any deposit from escrow and only after all claims to such deposit by the Buyer shall have been resolved by written agreement or final determination by a court competent jurisdiction and all appeals, if any, have been decided. Seller will then pay Broker six percent (6%) of the retained deposit after deduction of any attorneys' fees that may be incurred.

If the above is in accordance with your understanding, you will please note your acceptance thereof by signing and returning to us the duplicate copy of this letter.

Sincerely,

_____

President
(name of brokerage company)

AGREED AND ACCEPTED:

_____

RESIDENTIAL SALES AGREEMENT

Date: _____

Re: _____
(address of property)

Dear Mr. _____,

Pursuant to our understanding, you have, starting this day, appointed our firm to act as your sole agent, with the exclusive right to sell the apartments in the building(s) listed in Exhibit A.

It is our understanding that we may offer the apartments for sale to prospective purchasers and if, as, and when a sale of an apartment is consummated, and title has passed, you shall pay this firm a commission in a sum that equals six percent (6%) of the actual selling price.

During the course of this exclusive agreement, the following marketing strategies will be employed:

1. Signs will be affixed to the front of the buildings.
2. Advertising in *The New York Times* Sunday Classified Section will be placed on a continuing basis.
3. Ads will be placed in *The Wall Street Journal* every two weeks.
4. Photographs will be placed in *The New York Times* Sunday Magazine.
5. Photographs will be placed in Quest.
6. Open houses will be given for brokers on a continuing basis to ensure that the entire brokerage community has the opportunity to preview the properties.
7. The listings will be shared immediately with the entire brokerage community, and all price changes as well as pertinent information will be shared so as to keep brokers current on the status of the properties.
8. Telephone and mailing canvassing will be done to inform the neighborhood of the availability of the properties.

9. The properties will be listed within the relocation network at XYZ Real Estate, Inc., which offers a comprehensive marketing program designed to effect a profitable and timely sale of the apartments. Our Corporate Relocation Services Division receives referrals of qualified, New York–bound buyers from major corporations and our affiliate real estate firms nationwide.

10. An in-depth mailing to our large computerized customer base.

11. Inclusion on our Internet Marketing System with a subscription base of over 20 million people.

12. It is further understood by us that if the closing is not consummated for any cause or reason whatsoever after a contract of sale has been executed, except due to the willful default of the Seller, the commission set forth above is not due and payable, and we shall not have any claim whatsoever against you for a commission, or other compensation, in connection with this transaction.

This Exclusive Right to Sell agreement is in effect until _____. On the day of termination, we shall deliver to you a list of all prospective purchasers with whom we were negotiating and who theretofore visited the properties. If after the date of termination the properties are sold to individuals on said list, we shall receive from you the commission provided for above, as though such transaction had been consummated during the term of this agreement.

For purposes of this Agreement the term "_____," shall be deemed to include its affiliates, subsidiaries, parent company, nominees, successors, assigns, and/or any partnership or entity in which the undersigned or any general partner of the undersigned is a partner or principal.

This agreement shall be binding upon our successors and assigns.

If the above meets with your approval, kindly note your acceptance by signing and returning to us the duplicate copy of this letter.

We thank you for the confidence you have shown in us by placing this matter in our hands, and we assure you that it will receive our very best attention.

Very truly yours,

_____

John Smith, President
XYZ Real Estate, Inc.

AGREED AND ACCEPTED

_____

Source: © George F. Donohue

SAMPLE FORM FOR PURCHASING PROPERTY

Re: Offer to Purchase Building
   (Address)

Dear Mr. _____:

On behalf of _____, I am authorized to submit the following Offer to Purchase for the Seller's consideration.

1. **BUILDING:**   (City, State) _____

2. **SELLER:**

3. **PURCHASER:**

4. **PURCHASE PRICE:**   _____all cash. No mortgage or development contingencies.

5. **EARNEST MONEY DEPOSIT & DOWN PAYMENT:**
   $_____ (1% of the Purchase Price) to be delivered to an Escrow Agent acceptable to both Seller and Purchaser upon receipt of Seller's written acceptance of this offer and upon execution of a Purchase & Sale Contract.

A Down Payment of U.S. $_____ (4% of the Purchase Price) shall be deposited in the same escrow account. The Earnest Money Deposit and Down Payment shall be refundable if the transaction fails to close for any reason except for Purchaser's willful default. The Earnest Money Deposit shall be held in escrow in an interest-bearing account by the Escrow Agent, with interest credited to Purchaser at closing. Closing expenses and contingencies to be defined in Purchase & Sale Contract, at closing.

6. **DUE DILIGENCE PERIOD:**   Sixty (60) days. Commencing at the execution of a Purchase & Sale Contract.

7. **CLOSING DATE:**   Within thirty (30) days after due diligence period.

8. **CONDITION OF THE PROPERTY:**
   The Seller shall deliver the property to the Purchaser in an "as-is" basis, without any representations with reference to any physical condition other than the delivery of the base building "core and shell" systems. The property shall be delivered in "good repair and working order" at closing by Seller. The Purchaser shall confirm the condition of the property during the due diligence period by an investigative evaluation performed by a licensed professional engineer, to be employed by the Purchaser, at its sole cost and expense.

9. **LEASE DOCUMENTS/OPERATING STATEMENT REVIEW:**
   The Seller shall make all information relating to the Property, including but not limited to existing lease documents and other annual operating statements, available for review by the Purchaser, its agents, and consultants, prior to the closing of the proposed sale of the Property.

10. **HAZARDOUS, TOXIC, AND/OR ASBESTOS CONTAINING MATERIALS ("ACM") CONDITION:**
    The Seller shall be obligated to deliver the subject Property to the Purchaser free of any hazardous, toxic, and/or asbestos-containing materials ("ACM").

11. BROKERAGE COMMISSION:

This offer is submitted on the basis that one (1) full commission, in the amount of $_____, or ____% of the Purchase Price, shall be paid in full to _____, Principal Broker for this transaction, by the Seller at closing.

12. PURCHASE & SALE CONTRACT:

The parties shall enter into a Purchase & Sale Contract mutually satisfactory to them and their respective counsel, which when executed, shall constitute the sole and binding agreement between the parties hereto.

13. CONDITION:

This letter is an offer and neither party shall have any legal obligations to the other unless and until a binding Purchase & Sale Contract is executed between the parties. This offer is intended solely for the purpose of setting forth the basic terms to be contained in the Purchase & Sale Contract if the parties are able to reach a final agreement. The execution of a Purchase & Sale Contract in a form satisfactory to both parties and their respective counsel is an express condition precedent to the obligations of either party with respect to the proposed sale of the Property.

14. ADDITIONAL REMARKS:

The Purchaser's corporate profile to be provided.

If you have any questions or need further information, please contact me at your earliest convenience. Thank you very much for your attention in regard to this matter.

Sincerely,

_____(your name)

Accepted by: _____

Title: _____

As of this date: _____

Source: © George F. Donohue

D

SAMPLE REAL ESTATE MANAGEMENT CONTRACT

REAL ESTATE MANAGEMENT AGREEMENT

Between_____, Owner, and_____, Manager.

THIS AGREEMENT dated as of the ____ of _____, 200__, by and between _____, as principal (hereinafter collectively referred to as "Owner"), and _____, a Corporation chartered in the State of _____, hereinafter referred to as "Manager," as agent, shall be in effect for a period of two years from date.

WITNESSETH

WHEREAS, Owner owns the tracts of real estate legally described in "Exhibit A" attached hereto and made a part hereof; and

WHEREAS, Owner desires to appoint Manager as Owner's agent to handle, manage, and control the real estate;

NOW THEREFORE, in consideration of the premises and the mutual promises and covenants herein contained, Owner and Manager agree as follows:

ARTICLE I

Powers and Duties of the Manager

1.01   Owner hereby appoints Manager as Owner's agent to handle, manage, and control THE PROPERTIES, and expressly authorizes and empowers Manager as follows:

(a) To advertise THE PROPERTIES for lease and to execute leases covering THE PROPERTIES, or any part thereof, for such rent and upon such terms and conditions as Manager may deem wise and proper, PROVIDED, HOWEVER, that Manager shall not enter into a lease for a period longer than _____ years from the beginning date of such lease without Owner's written consent. Advertising is an operating expense and will be charged to the building. Advertising will be capped at $_____ per _____.

(b) To collect the rents and revenues from THE PROPERTIES.

(c) To maintain and keep THE PROPERTIES in a reasonable state of repair and to expend such part of the rents and revenues from THE PROPERTIES, which it collects, as may be necessary in so doing; PROVIDED, HOWEVER, Manager shall not spend more than $_____ in repairing any one tract of real estate (or the improvements thereon) constituting THE PROPERTIES during any 12-month period unless and until first receiving the written consent of Owner to do so.

(d) To keep the improvements of THE PROPERTIES insured against the hazards normally covered by fire and extended-coverage insurance policies and rental income insurance and public liability insurance policies in such amounts as Manager may determine to be adequate to protect the interest of Owner.

(e) To pay ad valorem taxes and improvement assessments against THE PROPERTIES before same become delinquent.

(f) To maintain out of the rents and revenues collected from THE PROPERTIES such reserves as Manager may deem wise and proper.

(g) To employ such attorneys, agents, contractors, and workmen as Manager may deem wise and proper in connection with the handling, managing, and control of THE PROPERTIES.

(h) The Manager will be responsible for the hiring and firing of maintenance personnel.

(i) To adjust and compromise any claim that may be asserted with respect to THE PROPERTIES and/or that may arise in connection with the management of THE PROPERTIES and to give binding releases in connection therewith.

(j) Generally, to handle, manage, and control THE PROPERTIES and to execute such agreements, contracts, or other documents or do such other acts or things as Manager, from time to time, may deem wise and proper to carry out the duties stated in this Agreement.

1.02 Manager shall keep proper books of account of this agency, which said books shall be open to inspection by Owner during the regular business hours of the Manager. Manager need not maintain segregated bank accounts relating to Owner. Owner hereby appoints Manager as Owner's agent to handle, manage, and control THE PROPERTIES, but the books and records shall reflect at all times the rents and revenues received and the disbursements made as to each tract of real estate comprising THE PROPERTIES. Accounts shall be kept in compliance with all applicable state laws. At such periodic intervals as Owner shall request, but not more frequently than monthly, Manager shall furnish to Owner a statement showing the rents and revenues received, the disbursements made, and the other transactions had with respect to THE PROPERTIES for the period indicated by Owner.

1.03 Manager may continue to hold THE PROPERTIES to be handled, managed, and controlled in accordance with the terms and conditions of this Agreement without liability or depreciation or loss, and the

1.04 Manager is not authorized by this Agreement either to make any capital improvements on THE PROPERTIES or to sell any of the real estate constituting a part of THE PROPERTIES, unless and until first instructed in writing by Owner to do so.

1.05   Owner agrees that Manager shall be under no duty to undertake any action, other than as herein specified, with respect to the handling, managing, and controlling of THE PROPERTIES, unless and until specifically agreed to in writing by Manager.

1.06   Owner agrees that Manager shall have a lien against THE PROPERTIES to secure the payment of Manager's compensation and any advances Manager may make from the other funds.

1.07   Owner's objectives in the management of this property are:

_____

_____

_____

1.08   Owner shall be responsible for the payment of:

(a) Payroll

(b) Insurance. Owner shall carry sufficient liability and various compensation insurance. Owner shall furnish certificate of evidence.

(c) Purchasing. Owner shall give Manager a schedule of payments for debt service, taxes, insurance, and other expenses so Manager can establish a budget.

(d) Owner will be responsible for the payment of repairs and maintenance and compliance of lease terms.

Manager shall manage THE PROPERTIES accordingly.

ARTICLE II

Rights Reserved by the Parties

2.01   This Agreement may be altered, amended, or modified at any time by a written mutual Agreement, signed by Owner and Manager.

2.02   This Agreement may be terminated by either Owner or Manager giving to the other at least ninety (90) days' written notice of intention to terminate this Agreement on a certain date specified in such notice; PROVIDED, HOWEVER, the termination of this Agreement shall not affect the right of Manager to receive leasing commissions or fees that have accrued on the date specified in such notice and have not been paid.

ARTICLE III

Manager's Compensation and Right of Reimbursement

3.01   For service hereunder, Manager shall be entitled to receive five percent (5%) of the gross income.

Payment to be made monthly. A minimum fee of $10,000 per month in advance will be paid monthly.

3.02   Owner promises and agrees to indemnify Manager and hold Manager harmless from and against any and all losses and liabilities incurred by Manager as a result of any action in good faith taken or not taken by Manager pursuant to the terms and conditions of this Agreement. The promise and agreement of Owner contained in this paragraph 3.02 shall survive any termination of this Agreement as to any such action taken or not taken by Manager prior to the receipt of Manager of written notice of such termination.

ARTICLE IV

Miscellaneous

4.01   This Agreement shall be binding upon and shall inure to the benefit of Owner and Manager and their respective heirs, executors, administrators, successors, and assigns.

4.02   All notices authorized or required between the parties or required by any provision of this Lease or by law shall be in writing and must be received by the parties or delivered by receipted means to the notification address of the receiving part, as set forth below, or to such other address as the parties may direct by notice given as herein provided. The effective date of any notice given hereunder shall be the date on which such notice is received or delivered as above set forth.

NOTIFICATION ADDRESSES

Owner   Manager

ARTICLE V

Special Terms and Conditions
(Insert any special provisions relating to this particular relationship and/or THE PROPERTIES.)

ARTICLE VI

Distribution of Income

6.01   Manager shall distribute the "net income" as that term is hereinafter defined, derived from the handling, managing, and controlling of THE PROPERTIES to Owner in accordance with the written instructions of Owner at such intervals, not more frequently than monthly, as Owner may state in said written instructions. "Net income," as used in this paragraph, means gross rents and revenues derived from THE PROPERTIES after deducting proper expenses and amounts requisite for maintenance of authorized reserves.

IN WITNESS WHEREOF, Owner and Manager have executed this Agreement, as of the date first above written.

Owner: _____
                President

Manager: _____
                President

Owner Contact: _____
                        Name   Telephone

Manager Contact: _____
                          Name   Telephone

"EXHIBIT A"

List of Owner's Properties to Be Managed by Manager

Source: © George F. Donohue

E

SAMPLE "GOOD GUY" GUARANTEE FORM

"GOOD GUY" GUARANTEE

The purpose of this Limited Guarantee is to assure the Landlord that during any period that Tenant is in possession of the Demised Premises, the payment of all rent and additional rent shall be made.

1. The "Surrender Date" shall be the date that is prior to or subsequent to the Expiration Date specified in the Lease (as defined herein) and that Tenant (as defined herein) shall have performed all of the following: (a) vacated and surrendered the Demised Premises (as defined herein) to Landlord (as defined herein) free of all subleases or licensees and in broom-clean condition, (b) so notified Landlord or such agent in writing, and (c) delivered the keys to the Demised Premises to Landlord (or its managing agent). Guarantor shall *not* be liable under this Guarantee for any rent, additional rent, or other charges or payments accruing under the Lease *after the Surrender Date*.

2. As an inducement to ("Landlord") to enter into a lease dated as of _____, 200__ ("Lease") with _____, a _____ corporation ("Tenant"), of premises located

on the _____Floor of _____, New York, New York (the "Demised Premises") the undersigned (the "Guarantor") hereby guarantees to Landlord all rent and additional rent payable by Tenant under the Lease ("Accrued Rent") up to the Surrender Date.

3.   Any security deposit under the Lease shall not be credited against amounts payable by Tenant, or by Guarantor, under the terms of this Guarantee. The acceptance of a surrender of the Demised Premises shall not be deemed a release or waiver by Landlord of any obligation of the Tenant under the Lease.

4.   This Guarantee is absolute and unconditional and is a guarantee of payment and performance, not of collection, and Guarantor's liability hereunder shall be primary. This Guarantee may be enforced without the necessity of resorting to or exhausting any other security or remedy, without the necessity at any time of having recourse to Tenant, and without having commenced any action against or having obtained any judgment against Tenant or Guarantor. The validity of this Guarantee shall not be affected or impaired by reason of the assertion by Landlord against Tenant of any of the rights or remedies reserved to Landlord under the Lease. Guarantor agrees that this Guarantee shall remain in force and effect as to any assignment, transfer, renewal, modification, or extension of the Lease. No action of Landlord or Tenant shall affect the obligations of Guarantor hereunder. The Guarantor waives notice of any and all defaults by Tenant in the payment of annual rent, additional rent, or other charges, and waives notice of any and all defaults by Tenant in performance of any of the terms of the Lease on Tenant's part to be performed.

5.   If Tenant becomes insolvent or shall be adjudicated a bankrupt or shall file for reorganization or similar relief or if such petition is filed by creditors of Tenant, under any present or future Federal or State law or if the Lease is terminated or Tenant's obligations otherwise discharged in any bankruptcy proceeding, Guarantor's obligations hereunder may nevertheless be enforced against the Guarantor.

6.   This Guarantee shall be governed by, and construed in accordance with, the laws of the State of New York. Guarantor hereby waives any right to trial by jury in any action or proceeding arising out of this Guarantee and will pay attorneys' fees, court costs, and other expenses incurred by Landlord in enforcing or attempting to enforce this Guarantee.

All terms and provisions herein shall inure to the benefit of the assigns and successors of Landlord and shall be binding upon the assigns and successors of Guarantor.

IN WITNESS WHEREOF, the Guarantor has signed this Guarantee on the _____ day of _____, 200__.

_____

Signature   Social Security Number

STATE OF NEW YORK   )
)
COUNTY OF NEW YORK   )

On the _____ day of _____, 200__ before me personally came _____, to me known and known to me to be the individual described in and who executed the foregoing Guarantee, and he/she duly acknowledged to me that he/she executed the same.

_____

                         Notary Public

Source: © George F. Donohue

SAMPLE FINANCIAL
STATEMENT

SAMPLE FINANCIAL STATEMENT

As of .... 200.........

NAME			BUSINESS (NAME OF EMPLOYER AND ADDRESS		
HOME ADDRESS			POSITION		BUSINESS TELEPHONE
HOME TELEPHONE	AGE	NO. OF DEPENDENTS	AGE(S) OF DEPENDENTS	YEARS WITH PRESENT EMPLOYER	GROSS FACE VALUE OF LIFE INSURANCE

ASSETS		LIABILITIES AND NET WORTH	
Cash		Notes payable to banks:	
		Secured	
U.S. Government securities		Unsecured	
Other marketable securities		Other notes payable	
Nonmarketable securities		Accounts and bills payable (Including credit cards and other installment payments)	
Real estate—estimated mkt. value (original cost $_____)		Mortgages payable	
Notes and mortgages		Unpaid taxes	
Cash value of life insurance			
Personal property (describe briefly)		Other debts (describe briefly)	
Other assets (describe briefly)			
		TOTAL LIABILITIES	
		NET WORTH	
TOTAL ASSETS		**TOTAL LIABILITIES & NET WORTH**	

ANNUAL INCOME

Salary (last year
$_____) _____

Drawings from partnerships
or proprietorships _____

Other Income (describe
source) _____

_____

_____

_____

_____

_____

TOTAL ANNUAL INCOME _____

Estimated income after
income taxes _____

ESTIMATED ANNUAL EXPENSES

Rent or mortgage (include
property tax, co-op, or
condominium
maintenance payments, etc.) _____

Alimony/child support _____

Life Insurance payments _____

Tuition payments _____

All other _____

TOTAL: _____

CONTINGENT LIABILITIES

Endorser _____

Tax claims _____

Litigation _____

Other _____

TOTAL _____

NAME OF SECURITES OWNED (GOVERNMENT SECURITIES)	NUMBER OF SHARES AND/OR FACE VALUE OF BONDS	IN NAME OF	CURRENT MARKET VALUE	CURRENT MARKET PRICE PER SHARE
			$ _____	_____
_____	_____	_____	_____	_____
_____	_____	_____	_____	_____
(MARKETABLE)				
_____	_____	_____	_____	_____
_____	_____	_____	_____	_____
(NONMARKETABLE)				
_____	_____	_____	_____	_____
_____	_____	_____	_____	_____
_____	_____	_____	_____	_____

PLEASE INDICATE BY * ANY OF THE ABOVE ASSETS THAT ARE PLEDGED

NOTES AND MORTGAGES OWNED	TOTAL YEARLY AMORTIZATION, IF ANY	RATE	DUE	AMOUNT
				$ _____
_____	_____	_____	_____	_____
_____	_____	_____	_____	_____

REAL ESTATE OWNED	IN NAME OF	OUTSTANDING MORTGAGE	RATE	DUE	MARKET VALUE
_____	_____	_____	_____	___ _	$ _____
_____	_____	_____	_____	_____	_____
_____	_____	_____	_____	_____	_____

BANK NOTES AND OTHER DEBTS PAYABLE	TOTAL YEARLY AMORTIZATION, IF ANY	RATE	DUE	AMOUNT
_____	_____	_____	_____	_____
_____	_____	_____	_____	_____
_____	_____	_____	_____	_____
_____	_____	_____	_____	_____

DATE: _____   _____
                                            SIGNATURE

Source: © George F. Donohue

ROLE-PLAYING SCRIPTS

These scripts complement the role-playing scripts found in Chapter 15. Refer to that chapter for instructions.

SCRIPT NUMBER ONE—THE MANAGER

You are a manager of a company and an employee has come to you seeking a raise. Your situation is as follows:

- The employee is a good worker and loyal.
- The employee's absenteeism is higher than average.
- Your budget only allows for a 3 percent raise when the employee deserves it.
- Specific reasons must be given for the raise.
- This employee is a good candidate for a promotion.

You could easily replace this employee, but you do not want the employee to quit.

SCRIPT NUMBER TWO—THE BUYER

You found a great property for sale and definitely want to buy it. Your situation is as follows:

- You're not sure if the seller wants to sell the property.
- The price ($520,000) is too high for you.
- Values are going up and you want to buy it at a good price.
- You know the property needs about $50,000 worth of renovation.
- You only have $80,000 for the down payment.
- The highest you'll go is $475,000.

SCRIPT NUMBER THREE—THE TENANT

You own a successful sandwich/coffee shop franchise and are seeking to lease retail space. Your situation is as follows:

- Rents seem to be heading downward.
- There are many other retail spaces available in the marketplace.
- This is the only corner space.
- This corner location would be ideal for a new store.
- The asking price is $50 per square foot per year, however, you can only afford to pay less than or equal to 15 percent of your projected gross income, which equates to $45 per square foot per year.
- You can open the store any time within the next six months.
- You notice the space needs repairs.
- You prefer not to pay a security deposit.

Source: © George F. Donohue

A

abstract of title   A summary of all of the recorded instruments and proceedings that affect the title to property, arranged in the order in which they were recorded

accretion   The addition of land through processes of nature, as by water or wind

accrued interest   Accrue; to grow; to be added to. Accrued interest is interest that has been earned but not due and payable.

acknowledgment   A formal declaration before a duly authorized officer by a person who has executed an instrument that such execution is the person's act and deed

acquisition   An act or process by which a person procures property

acre   A measure of land equaling 43,560 square feet

action for specific performance   A court action to compel a defaulting principal to comply with the provisions of a contract

adjacent   Lying near to but not necessarily in actual contact with

adjoining   Contiguous; attaching, in actual contact with

administrator   A person appointed by the court to administer the estate of a deceased person who left no will; i.e., who died intestate

ad valorem   According to valuation

adverse possession   A means of acquiring title where an occupant has been in actual, open, notorious, exclusive, and continuous occupancy of property under a claim of right for the required statutory period

affidavit   A statement or declaration reduced to writing and sworn to or affirmed before some officer who is authorized to administer an oath or affirmation

affirm   To confirm, to ratify, to verify

agency That relationship between principal and agent that arises out of a contract either expressed or implied, written or oral, wherein an agent is employed by a person to do certain acts on the person's behalf in dealing with a third party

agent One who undertakes to transact some business or to manage some affair for another by authority of the latter

agreement of sale A written agreement between seller and purchaser in which the purchaser agrees to buy certain real estate and the seller agrees to sell upon terms and conditions set forth therein

air rights Rights in real property to use the space above the surface of the land

alienation A transferring of property to another; the transfer of property and possession of lands, or other things, from one person to another

alienation clause Allows a lender to require the balance of a loan to be paid in full if the collateral is sold (also known as a "due on sale" clause)

amortization A gradual paying off of a debt by periodic installments

apportionment Adjustment of the income, expenses, or carrying charges of real estate usually computed to the date of closing of title so that the seller pays all expenses to that date. The buyer assumes all expenses commencing the date the deed is conveyed to the buyer.

appraisal An estimate of a property's value by an appraiser who is usually presumed to be expert in his or her work

appraisal by cost approach Adding together all parts of a property separately appraised to form a whole; e.g., the value of the land considered as vacant added to the cost of reproduction of the building, less depreciation

appraisal by income capitalization approach An estimate of value by capitalization of productivity and income

appraisal by sale comparison approach Comparability with the sales prices of other similar properties

appurtenance Something that is outside the property itself but belongs to the land and adds to its greater enjoyment, such as a right-of-way or a barn or a dwelling

assessed valuation A valuation placed upon property by a public officer or a board, as a basis for taxation

assessment   A charge against real estate made by a unit of government to cover a proportionate cost of an improvement, such as a street or sewer

assessor   An official who has the responsibility of determining assessed values

assignee   The person to whom an agreement or contract is assigned

assignment   The method or manner by which a right or contract is transferred from one person to another

assignor   A party who assigns or transfers an agreement or contract to another

assumption of mortgage   The taking of title to property by a grantee, wherein the grantee assumes liability for payment of an existing note or bond secured by a mortgage against a property and becomes personally liable for the payment of such mortgage debt

avulsion   A sudden and perceptible loss or addition to land by the action of water, or a sudden change in the bed or course of a stream

B

balloon mortgage payment   A large payment during the term of a mortgage, often at the end

beneficiary   The person who receives or is to receive the benefits resulting from certain acts

bequeath   To give or hand down by will; to leave by will

bequest   That which is given by the terms of a will

bill of sale   A written instrument given to pass title of personal property from vendor to vendee

binder   An agreement to cover the down payment for the purchase of real estate as evidence of good faith on the part of the purchaser

blanket mortgage   A mortgage covering more than one property. A blanket mortgage is often used for subdivision financing.

blockbusting   The practice of inducing homeowners in a particular neighborhood to sell their homes quickly, often at below market prices, by creating the fear that the entry of a minority group or groups into the neighborhood will cause a precipitous decline in property values

bona fide   In good faith, without fraud

bond   The evidence of a personal debt that is secured by a mortgage or other lien on real estate

building code   Regulations established by state or local governments stating fully the structural requirements for building

building line   A line fixed at a certain distance from the front and/or sides of a lot, beyond which no building can project

building loan agreement   An agreement whereby the lender advances money to an owner primarily in the erection of buildings. Such funds are commonly advanced in installments as the structure is completed.

building permit   Written governmental permission for the construction, renovation, or substantial repair of a building

C

cancellation clause   A provision in a lease or other contract that confers upon one or more of all of the parties to the lease the right to terminate the party's or parties' obligations thereunder upon the occurrence of the condition or contingency set forth in the said clause

capital appreciation   The appreciation accruing to the benefit of the capital improvement to real estate

capital asset   Any asset of a permanent nature used for the production of income

capital gain   Income that results from the sale of an asset not in the usual course of business. (Capital gains may be taxed at a lower rate than ordinary income.)

capital improvement   Any structure erected as a permanent improvement to real estate, usually extending the useful life and value of a property. (The replacement of a roof would be considered a capital improvement.)

capital loss   A loss from the sale of an asset not in the usual course of business

caveat emptor   Let the buyer beware. The buyer must examine the goods or property and buy at the buyer's own risk.

cease and desist list   Upon the establishment of a cease and desist zone by the Secretary, a list of homeowners who have filed owner's statements expressing their wish not to be solicited by real estate brokers or salespersons. Soliciting of listed homeowners by licensees is prohibited. Violators of such prohibition are subject to licensure suspension or revocation.

cease and desist zone   A rule adopted by the Secretary of State that prohibits the direct solicitation of homeowners whose names and addresses appear on a cease and desist list maintained by the Secretary. Such rule may be adopted upon the Secretary's determination that some homeowners within a defined geographic area have been subject to intense and repeated solicitation by real estate brokers and salespersons.

certificate of occupancy (CO)   A document issued by a governmental authority that a building is ready and fit for occupancy

chain of title   A history of conveyances and encumbrances affecting a title from the time the original patent was granted, or as far back as records are available

chattel   Personal property, such as household goods

client   The one by whom a broker is employed

closing date   The date upon which the property is conveyed by the seller to the buyer

cloud on the title   An outstanding claim or encumbrance that, if valid, would affect or impair the owner's title

collateral   Additional security pledged for the payment of an obligation

color of title   That which appears to be good title, but that is not title in fact

commingling   To mingle or mix, for example, a client's funds in the broker's personal or general account

commission   A sum due a real estate broker for services in that capacity

commitment   A pledge or a promise; affirmation agreement

completion bond   A bond used to guarantee that a proposed subdivision development will be completed

condemnation   Taking private property for public use, with fair compensation to the owner; exercising the right of eminent domain

conditional sales contract   A contract for the sale of property stating that delivery is to be made to the buyer, title to remain vested in the seller until the conditions of the contract have been fulfilled

consideration   Anything given to induce another to enter into a contract, such as money or personal services

constructive notice Information or knowledge of a fact imputed by law to a person because the person could have discovered the fact by proper diligence and inquiry (e.g., via public records)

contingency A provision in a contract that requires the occurrence of a specific event before the contract can be completed

contract An agreement between competent parties to do or not to do certain things that is legally enforceable, whereby each party acquires a right

conversion Change from one character or use to another

conveyance The transfer of the title of land from one to another; the means or medium by which title of real estate is transferred

covenants Agreements written into deeds and other instruments promising performance or nonperformance of certain acts, or stipulating certain uses or nonuses of the property

cul-de-sac A blind alley; a street with only one outlet

current value The value usually sought to be estimated in an appraisal

D

damages The indemnity recoverable by a person who has sustained an injury, either to his or her person, property, or relative rights, through the act or default of another

debit The amount charged as due or owed

duress Unlawful constraint exercised upon a person whereby the person is forced to do some act against the person's will

E

earnest money Down payment made by a purchaser of real estate as evidence of good faith

easement A right that may be exercised by the public or individuals on, over, or through the lands of others

economic life The period over which a property will yield the investor a return on the investment

economic obsolescence Lessened desirability or useful life arising from economic forces, such as changes in optimum land use, legislative enactments that restrict or impair property rights, and changes in supply-demand ratios

ejectment A form of action to regain possession of real property, with damages for the unlawful retention; used when there is no relationship of landlord and tenant

eminent domain A right of the government to acquire property for necessary public use by condemnation; the owner must be fairly compensated

encroachment A building, part of a building, or obstruction that intrudes upon or invades a highway or sidewalk or trespasses upon the property of another

encumbrance Any right to or interest in the land interfering with its use or transfer, or subjecting it to an obligation (Also *incumbrance*)

endorsement An act of signing one's name on the back of a check or note, with or without further qualifications

equity The interest or value that the owner has in real estate over and above the liens against it

equity loan Junior loan based on a percentage of the equity

equity of redemption A right of the owner to reclaim property before it is sold through foreclosure proceedings, by the payment of the debt, interest, and costs

erosion The wearing away of land through processes of nature, as by water and winds

escheat The reversion to the State of property in the event the owner thereof abandons it or dies, without leaving a will and has no distributees to whom the property may pass by lawful descent

escrow A written agreement between two or more parties providing that certain instruments or property be placed with a third party to be delivered to a designated person upon the fulfillment or performance of some act or condition

estate The degree, quantity, nature, and extent of interest that a person has in real property

estate at will The occupation of lands and tenements by a tenant for an indefinite period, terminable by one or both parties at will

estate in reversion The residue of an estate left for the grantor, to commence in possession after the termination of some particular estate granted by the grantor

estoppel certificate An instrument executed by the mortgagor setting forth the present status and the balance due on the mortgage as of the date of the execution of the certificate

eviction   A legal proceeding by a landlord to recover possession of real property from a tenant

eviction, actual   Where one is, either by force or by process of law, actually put out of possession

eviction, constructive   Any disturbance of the tenant's possession of the leased premises by the landlord whereby the premises are rendered unfit or unsuitable for the purpose for which they were leased

exclusive agency   An agreement of employment of a broker to the exclusion of all other brokers; if sale is made by any other broker during term of employment, broker holding exclusive agency is entitled to commissions in addition to the commissions payable to the broker who *effected* the transaction

exclusive right to sell   An agreement of employment by a broker under which the exclusive right to sell for a specified period is granted to the broker; if a sale during the term of the agreement is made by the owner or by any other broker, the broker holding such exclusive right to sell is nevertheless entitled to compensation

executor   A male person or a corporate entity or any other type of organization named or designed in a will to carry out its provisions as to the disposition of the estate of a deceased person

executrix   A woman appointed to perform the same duties as an executor

extension agreement   An agreement that extends the life of a mortgage to a later date

F

fee; fee simple; fee absolute   Absolute ownership of real property; a person has this type of estate where the person is entitled to the entire property with unconditional power of disposition during the person's life and descending to the person's heirs or distributees

fiduciary   A person who, on behalf of or for the benefit of another, transacts business or handles money or property not the person's own; such relationship implies great confidence and trust

fixtures   Personal property so attached to the land or improvements as to become part of the real property

foreclosure   A procedure whereby property pledged as security for a debt is sold to pay the debt in the event of default in payments or terms

freehold An interest in real estate, not less than an estate for life. (Use of this term discontinued September 1, 1967.)

G

grace period Additional time allowed to perform an act or make a payment before a default occurs

graduated leases A lease that provides for a graduated change at stated intervals in the amount of the rent to be paid; used largely in long-term leases

grant A technical term used in deeds of conveyance of lands to indicate a transfer

grantee The party to whom the title to real property is conveyed

grantor The person who conveys real estate by deed; the seller

gross income Total income from property before any expenses are deducted

gross lease A lease of property whereby the lessor is to meet all property charges regularly incurred through ownership

ground rent Earnings of improved property credited to earnings of the ground itself after allowance made for earnings of improvements

group boycott An agreement between members of a trade to exclude other members from fair participation in the trade

H

habendum clause The "to have and to hold" clause that defines or limits the quantity of the estate granted in the premises of the deed

holdover tenant A tenant who remains in possession of leased property after the expiration of the lease term

I

incompetent A person who is unable to manage his or her own affairs by reason of insanity, imbecility, or feeblemindedness

in rem A proceeding against the realty directly; as distinguished from a proceeding against a person (Used in taking land for nonpayment of taxes, etc.)

installments   Parts of the same debt, payable at successive periods as agreed; payments made to reduce a mortgage

instrument   A written legal document; created to *effect* the rights of the parties

interest rate   The percentage of a sum of money charged for its use

intestate   A person who dies having made no will, or leaves one that is defective in form, in which case the person's estate descends to the person's distributees in the manner prescribed by law

involuntary lien   A lien imposed against property without consent of the owner, such as taxes, special assessments

irrevocable   Incapable of being recalled or revoked; unchangeable; unalterable

J

joint tenancy   Ownership of realty by two or more persons, each of whom has an undivided interest with the "right of survivorship"

judgment   A formal decision issued by a court concerning the respective rights and claims of the parties to an act or suit

junior mortgage   A mortgage second in lien to a previous mortgage

L

laches   Delay or negligence in asserting one's legal rights

landlord   One who rents property to another

lease   A contract whereby, for a consideration, usually termed rent, one who is entitled to the possession of real property transfers such rights to another for life, for a term of years, or at will

leasehold   The interest or estate that a lessee of real estate has therein by virtue of the lessee's lease

lessee   A person to whom property is rented under a lease

lessor   One who rents property to another under a lease

lien   A legal right or claim upon a specific property that attaches to the property until a debt is satisfied

life estate   The conveyance of title to property for the duration of the life of the grantee

life tenant   The holder of a life estate

lis pendens   A legal document, filed in the office of the county clerk, giving notice that an auction or proceeding is pending in the courts affecting the title to the property. (Not applicable in commission disputes.)

listing   An employment contract between principal and agent, authorizing the agent to perform services for the principal involving the latter's property

littoral rights   The right of a property owner whose land borders on a body of water, such as a lake, ocean, or sea, to reasonable use and enjoyment of the shore and water the property borders on

M

mandatory   Requiring strict conformity or obedience

marketable title   A title that a court of equity considers to be so free from defect that it will enforce its acceptance by a purchaser

market allocation   An agreement between members of a trade to refrain from competition in specific market areas

market price   The actual selling price of a property

market value   The most probable price that a property should bring if exposed for sale in the open market for a reasonable period of time, with both the buyer and seller aware of current market conditions, neither being under duress

mechanic's lien   A lien given by law upon a building or other improvement upon land, and upon the land itself, to secure the price of labor done upon, and materials furnished for, the improvement

meeting of the minds   Whenever all parties to a contract agree to the substance and terms thereof

metes and bounds   A term used in describing the boundary lines of land, seeing forth all the boundary lines together with their terminal points and angles

minor   A person under an age specified by law; usually under 18 years of age

monument   A fixed object and point established by surveyors to establish land locations

mortgage   An instrument in writing, duly executed and delivered, that creates a lien upon real estate as security for the payment of a specified debt, which is usually in the form of a bond

mortgage commitment   A formal indication by a lending institution that it will grant a mortgage loan on property in a certain specified amount and on certain specified terms

mortgagee   The party who lends money and takes a mortgage to secure the payment thereof

mortgage reduction certificate   An instrument executed by the mortgagee, setting forth the present status and the balance due on the mortgage as of the date of the execution of the instrument

mortgagor   A person who borrows money and gives a mortgage on the person's property as security for the payment of the debt

multiple listing   An arrangement among Real Estate Board of Exchange members, whereby each broker presents the broker's listings to the attention of the other members so that if a sale results, the commission is divided between the broker bringing the listing and the broker making the sale

N

net listing   A price below which an owner will not sell the property, and at which price a broker will not receive a commission; the broker receives the excess over and above the net listing as the broker's commission

nonsolicitation order   A rule adopted by the Secretary of State that prohibits any or all types of solicitation directed toward homeowners within a defined geographic area. Such rule may be adopted after a public hearing and upon the Secretary's determination that homeowners within the subject area have been subject to intense and repeated solicitations by real estate brokers or salespersons and that such solicitations have caused owners to reasonably believe that property values may decrease because persons of different race, ethnic, religious, or social backgrounds are moving or about to move into such area.

notary public   A public officer who is authorized to take acknowledgments to certain classes of documents, such as deeds, contracts, and mortgages, and before whom affidavits may be sworn

O

obligee   The person in whose favor an obligation is entered into

obligor The person who binds himself or herself to another; one who has engaged to perform some obligation; one who makes a bond

obsolescence Loss in value due to reduced desirability and usefulness of a structure because its design and construction become obsolete; loss because of becoming old fashioned, and not in keeping with modern means, with consequent loss of income

open listing A listing given to any number of brokers without liability to compensate any except the one who first secures a buyer ready, willing, and able to meet the terms of the listing, or secures the acceptance by the seller of a satisfactory offer; the sale of the property automatically terminates the listing

option A right given for a consideration to purchase or lease a property upon specified terms within a specified time; if the right is not exercised the option holder is not subject to liability for damages; if exercised, the grantor of option must perform

P

partition The division that is made of real property between those who own it in undivided shares

party wall A wall built along the line separating two properties, partly on each, which either owner, the owner's heirs, and assigns have the right to use; such right constituting an easement over so much of the adjoining owner's land as is covered by the wall

percentage lease A lease of property in which the rental is based upon the percentage of the volume of sales made upon the leased premises; usually provides for minimum rental

performance bond A bond used to guarantee the specific completion of an endeavor in accordance with a contract

personal property Any property that is not real property

plat book A public record containing maps of land showing the division of such land into streets, blocks, and lots, and indicating the measurements of the individual parcels

plottage Increment in unity value of a plot of land created by assembling smaller ownerships into one ownership

points Discount charges imposed by lenders to raise the yields on their loans

police power   The right of any political body to enact laws and enforce them, for the order, safety, health, morals, and general welfare of the public

power of attorney   A written instrument duly signed and executed by a person that authorizes an agent to act on his or her behalf to the extent indicated in the instrument

prepayment clause   A clause in a mortgage that gives a mortgagor the privilege of paying the mortgage indebtedness before it becomes due

price fixing   Conspiring to establish fixed fees or prices for services or products

principal   The employer of an agent or broker; the broker's or agent's client

probate   To establish the will of a deceased person

purchase money mortgage   A mortgage given by a grantee in part payment of the purchase price of real estate

Q

quiet enjoyment   The right of an owner or a person legally in possession to the use of property without interference of possession

quiet title suit   A suit in court to remove a defect, cloud, or suspicion regarding legal rights of an owner to a certain parcel of real property

quit claim deed   A deed that conveys simply the grantor's rights or interest in real estate, without any agreement or covenant as to the nature or extent of that interest, or any other covenants; usually used to remove a cloud from the title

R

racial steering   The unlawful practice of influencing a person's housing choice based on his or her race

real estate board   An organization whose members consist primarily of real estate brokers and salespersons

real estate syndicate   A partnership formed for participation in a real estate venture; partners may be limited or unlimited in their liability

realization of gain   The taking of the gain or profit from the sale of property

real property   Land, and generally whatever is erected upon or affixed thereto

Realtor   A coined word that may only be used by an active member of a local real estate board, affiliated with the National Association of Real Estate Boards

reconciliation   The final stage in the appraisal process when the appraiser reviews the data and estimates the subject property's value

recording   The act of writing or entering in a book of public record affecting the title to real property

recourse   The right to a claim against a prior owner of a property or note

redemption   The right of a mortgagor to redeem the property by paying a debt after the expiration date and before sale at foreclosure; the right of an owner to reclaim the owner's property after the sale for taxes

redlining   The refusal to lend money within a specific area for various reasons. This practice is illegal.

referee's deed   Used to convey real property sold pursuant to a judicial order, in an action for the foreclosure of a mortgage or for partition

release   The act or writing by which some claim or interest is surrendered to another

release clause   A clause found in a blanket mortgage that gives the owner of the property the privilege of paying off a portion of the mortgage indebtedness, and thus freeing a portion of the property from the mortgage

rem   (See *in rem.*)

remainder   An estate that takes effect after the termination of a prior estate, such as a life estate

remainderman   The person who is to receive the property after the termination of the prior estate

rent   The compensation paid for the use of real estate

reproduction cost   Normal cost of exact duplication of a property as of a certain date

restraint of trade   Business practices designed to restrict competition, create a monopoly, control prices, and otherwise obstruct the free operation of business

restriction   A limitation placed upon the use of property contained in the deed or other written instrument in the chain of title

reversionary interest   The interest that a grantor has in lands or other property upon the termination of the preceding estate

revocation   An act of recalling a power of authority conferred, as the revocation of a power of attorney; a license, an agency, etc.

right of survivorship   Right of the surviving joint owner to succeed to the interests of the deceased joint owner; distinguishing feature of a joint tenancy or tenancy by the entirety

right-of-way   The right to pass over another's land pursuant to an easement or license

riparian owner   One who owns land bounding upon a river or watercourse

riparian rights   The right of a property owner whose land borders a natural watercourse, such as a river, to reasonable use and enjoyment of the water that flows past the property. Riparian literally means "riverbank."

S

sales contract   A contract by which the buyer and seller agree to terms of sale

satisfaction piece   An instrument for recording and acknowledging payment of an indebtedness secured by a mortgage

second mortgage   A mortgage made by a homebuyer in addition to an existing first mortgage

seizin   The possession of land by one who claims to own at least an estate for life therein

setback   The distance from the curb or other established line, within which no buildings may be erected

situs   The location of a property

special assessment   An assessment made against a property to pay for a public improvement by which the assessed property is supposed to be especially benefited

specific performance   A remedy in a court of equity compelling a defendant to carry out the terms of an agreement or contract

statute   A law established by an act of the legislature

statute of frauds   State law that provides that certain contracts must be in writing to be enforceable at law

statute of limitations   A statute barring all right of action after a certain period from the time when a cause of action first arises

subagent   An agent of a person already acting as an agent of a principal

subdivision   A tract of land divided into lots or plots

subletting   A leasing by a tenant to another, who holds under the tenant

subordination clause   A clause that permits the placing of a mortgage at a later date that takes priority over an existing mortgage

subscribing witness   One who writes his or her name as witness to the execution of an instrument

surety   One who guarantees the performance of another; guarantor

surrender   The cancellation of a lease by mutual consent of the lessor and the lessee

surrogate's court (probate court)   A court having jurisdiction over the proof of wills, the settling of estates, and of citations

survey   The process by which a parcel of land is measured and its area ascertained; also the blueprint showing the measurements, boundaries, and area

T

tax sale   Sale of property after a period of nonpayment of taxes

tenancy at will   A license to use or occupy lands and tenements at the will of the owner

tenancy by the entirety   An estate that exists only between husband and wife with equal right of possession and enjoyment during their joint lives and with the "right of survivorship"

tenancy in common   An ownership of realty by two or more persons, each of whom has an undivided interest, without the "right of survivorship"

tenant   One who is given possession of real estate for a fixed period or at will

tenant at sufferance   One who comes into possession of land by lawful title and keeps it afterwards without any title at all

testate   Where a person dies leaving a valid will

tie-in arrangement   A contract where one transaction depends upon another

title   Evidence that owner of land is in lawful possession thereof; evidence of ownership

title insurance   A policy of insurance that indemnifies the holder for any loss sustained by reason of defects in the title

title search   An examination of the public records to determine the ownership and encumbrances affecting real property

Torrens title   System of title records provided by state law; it is a system for the registration of land titles whereby the state of the title, showing ownership and encumbrances, can be readily ascertained from an inspection of the "register of titles" without the necessity of a search of the public records

tort   A wrongful act, wrong, injury; violation of a legal right

transfer tax   A tax charged under certain conditions on the property belonging to an estate

U

urban property   City property; closely settled property

usury   On a loan, claiming a rate of interest greater than that permitted by law

V

valid   Having force, or binding force; legally sufficient and authorized by law

valuation   Estimated worth or price; the act of valuing by appraisal

variance   The authorization to improve or develop a particular property in a manner not authorized by zoning

vendee's lien   A lien against property under contract of sale to secure deposit paid by a purchaser

violations   Act, deed, or conditions contrary to law or permissible use of real property

void   To have no force or effect; that which is unenforceable

voidable   That which is capable of being adjudged void, but is not void unless action is taken to make it so

W

waiver   The renunciation, abandonment, or surrender of some claim, right, or privilege

warranty deed   A conveyance of land in which the grantor warrants the title to the grantee

water rights   The right of a property owner to use water on, under, or adjacent to the land for such purposes as irrigation, power, or private consumption

will   The disposition of one's property to take effect after death

wraparound loan   A new loan encompassing any existing loans

Z

zone   An area set off by the proper authorities for specific use; subject to certain restrictions or restraints

zoning ordinance   Act of city or county or other authorities specifying type and use to which property may be put in specific areas

Glossary compiled by George F. Donohue.

Renowned as a foremost negotiations expert, George F. Donohue has been involved with more real estate negotiations than most real estate professionals in the world today.

Donohue is the president of William B. May Commercial Real Estate, a division of William B. May, one of the leading real estate companies in the United States and the oldest real estate company in the United States (est. 1866). He has managed one of the largest real estate portfolios in the world, which included being head of real estate for the World Trade Center in New York City. Today, he is a corporate executive, author, professional speaker, consultant, professor, and television and radio spokesperson.

Donohue has earned an associate's degree in construction management, a bachelor's degree in architecture, and a master's of science degree in real estate development at New York University. He is currently a doctoral candidate in international business.

Over his lifetime, Donohue has taught the business of real estate and the art of negotiation to thousands of people. He consults with corporations, governments, and individuals worldwide, and is sought out by the media for his knowledge of real estate, architecture, and business. A well-known speaker—particularly in China, Japan, and Europe—his assignments have taken him to more than 40 countries around the globe.

During his career, Donohue has negotiated against numerous top executives and individuals from entities such as the Japanese, Russian, and French governments, Merrill Lynch, Bank of America, Dean Witter, The Commodities Exchange, the Society of Security Analysts, The Gap, JPMorgan Chase, Citibank, HSBC, Marsh and McLennan, Daiichi Kangyo Bank, Allstate Insurance, Bank of Tokyo, Bank of Taiwan, Duane Reade, McDonald's, Charles Schwab, and hundreds of others.

Share the message!

Bulk discounts
Discounts start at only 10 copies and range from 30% to 55% off retail price based on quantity.

Custom publishing
Private label a cover with your organization's name and logo. Or, tailor information to your needs with a custom pamphlet that highlights specific chapters.

Ancillaries
Workshop outlines, videos, and other products are available on select titles.

Dynamic speakers
Engaging authors are available to share their expertise and insight at your event.

**Call Dearborn Trade Special Sales at
1-800-621-9621, ext. 4444,
or e-mail trade@dearborn.com**